DESECRATION, DANGER, DELIVERANCE

WHAT THE BIBLE REALLY SAYS ABOUT THE RAPTURE

MARTIN WEBER

REVIEW AND HERALD® PUBLISHING ASSOCIATION
HAGERSTOWN, MD 21740

This book was
Edited by Richard W. Coffen
Copyedited by Delma Miller and James Cavil
Designed by Mark O'Connor
Electronic makeup by Shirley M. Bolivar
Cover photograph from PhotoDisc
Typeset: 11/12 Bembo

PRINTED IN U.S.A.

06 05 04 03 02   5 4 3 2 1

R&H Cataloging Service
Weber, Martin Herbert, 1951-
    Desecration, danger, deliverance: The deadly deception of
the secret rapture.

    1. Second Advent.   2. Rapture (Christian eschatology).
I. Title.

236

ISBN 0-8280-1706-9

CONTENTS

Other books by Martin Weber:

Who's Got the Truth?

To order, call 1-800-765-6955.

Visit us at www.reviewandherald.com for information on other Review and Herald® products.

Chapter 1

DEADLY DECEPTION

M issiles whistle through the sky. San Francisco explodes in flames. Chicago and other cities crumble.

A massive earthquake and its aftershocks rumble through the rubble of what's left. Tornadoes of turmoil swirl everywhere. One of every four people on Planet Earth is dead.

And all that happens before the *real* trouble starts.

Suddenly and ferociously, the great tribulation strikes. Antichrist Nicolae Carpathia, having died and risen again, now rules the world. From his global community headquarters in New Babylon, he wreaks carnage, demands worship, curses Christ, and does his devilish best to intimidate God's people. After brazenly breaking his covenant with Israel, Carpathia desecrates Jerusalem's new temple by shedding the blood of a pig on its altar. Human blood flows too as devastation and desolation multiply in New York, London, Rome—throughout the earth. False prophets populate the airwaves, promoting satanic propaganda on the 6:00 news.

Meanwhile, God is at work too. Led by 144,000 newly converted Jewish missionaries, the true church not only survives but actually thrives. From a laptop computer in his hideout, Messianic rabbi Tsion Ben-Judah communicates via the Internet with the world-wide flock. Rayford Steele; his daughter, Chloe; her husband, Buck; and the rest of the saints defy the persecution's guns and swords and guillotines. Many martyrs sacrifice their lives, but they die with shouts of triumph. Eager converts step forward to take their place.

Satan's strategy has backfired. He's furious, vowing revenge through Nicolae. Armageddon lurks around the corner.

Such is the incredible scenario of final events portrayed in the best-selling *Left Behind* books and movie. Is all of it actually biblical? Are you and your loved ones sufficiently prepared for earth's last hours? Better learn the truth so you can safeguard your future!

Let's get some background on what's happened so far in the story to bring us to this point.

The Rapture

Left Behind begins as an invisible flash sweeps through the world. Millions vanish. Men, women, teenagers, and every child on earth suddenly disappear, leaving everything—even the clothing they were wearing. Airplanes lose pilots; cars their drivers. The billions of bewildered souls left behind panic, plunging the earth into confusion and turmoil.

As days turn into weeks, life begins to assume normalcy again. Yet the question remains: What on earth happened? Some suspect kidnapping space aliens. Others discern an enemy attack from China or who knows where.

Rayford Steele knows better. His wife, now missing, had warned him and their 20-year-old daughter, Chloe, that Jesus would come suddenly and silently to rapture true believers. Everyone else would be left behind.

So it was. Rayford had been piloting a 747 over the ocean when the rapture happened. On board with him was gorgeous Hattie Durham, senior flight attendant, with whom he had been flirting. But now that he was left behind, it wasn't fun to flirt anymore.

Instead, Rayford embarks on a desperate search to discover the truth he once shunned regarding the rapture and other Bible prophecies. He remembers hearing about a second chance for anyone not ready for Jesus the first time. And so he and Chloe venture into church,, where they meet others also left behind. Assistant pastor Bruce Barnes, who confesses that he missed the rapture because of his superficial, phony faith, suddenly becomes the fearless and focused leader of his fellow new believers.

Tribulation Force

Rayford and Chloe find salvation at last. Together with Pastor Bruce they establish the "Tribulation Force"—a tiny but determined band of believers committed to do battle for God against satanic opposition during the upcoming seven-year Time of Tribulation. They determine to stand together, come what may, and never give in.

Joining them is Cameron "Buck" Williams, famous reporter for the news magazine *Global Weekly*. Assigned to get the facts about what happened in the disappearances, Buck makes the professional quest for truth his own spiritual search. Not only does he find faith in Jesus, but he also discovers the charms of Chloe. Despite second thoughts about whether romance is appropriate during the Tribulation, they fall in love and eventually get married.

Buck doesn't get to stay at home, though. The antichrist solicits his writing skills. Nicolae Carpathia is the most intriguing and mesmerizing political leader since Adolf Hitler. Within two weeks of the rapture, Carpathia had emerged as the leader of the United Nations. He enjoys the support of millions who trust his promise to unify the troubled planet into a peaceful global community.

Among those flocking to Nicolae Carpathia is flight attendant Hattie Durham, who becomes his personal assistant—very personal, in fact. Buck, being now a believer, feels terrible about this, since it was he who introduced Hattie to Nicolae. The Tribulation Force prays constantly for Hattie's deliverance and salvation.

There is much to pray about as the world plunges ever deeper into the Time of Tribulation. Nicolae solidifies his stranglehold on the Global Community— his new name for the United Nations. As its leader he pushes for a one-world currency and a one-world religion led by the pope of popes in Rome, Pontifex Maximus, Peter the Second.

In this "Enigma Babylon One World Church," the major world religions have formed an all-inclusive religion, uniting on common beliefs and swearing allegiance to Carpathia. Even the leaders of Israel are deceived into believing he is on their side. And so they enter into a covenant treaty with none other than the antichrist himself.

After three and a half years Nicolae suddenly breaks his covenant and prepares to desecrate Jerusalem's newly reconstructed temple. He now demands not just allegiance but worship for himself as deity and not just from Jews but from the whole world. His fierce quest for exclusive power plunges the world into the Great Tribulation. And that takes us back to where we started.

It's a thrilling story: war, intrigue, romance. *Left Behind* has it all. You may be one of many millions around the world for whom the men and women of the Trib Force are like family—Buck and Chloe, Chaim and Tsion, Rayford and David and Albie.

But several troubling questions emerge amid all the excitement surrounding this series. Is it possible that some readers have become more enthusiastic about the *Left Behind* fictional characters than they are about Jesus Himself? And do they know the *Left Behind* story line better than they know Bible prophecy? Do they even realize the difference between a religious novel and God's Word?

Something to think about. Maybe it's time to reach for our Bibles and do a reality check.

Perilous Confusion

Prophetic enthusiasm by itself is not enough. Back in the days of Jesus, people got so caught up in prophetic excitement about the promised Messiah that they forgot to open God's Word and make sure their expectations were accurately grounded. In fact, misconceptions about Bible prophecy led many sincere people to reject Jesus. They expected Christ to be a political as well as religious leader. They focused their attention upon Jerusalem, expecting their Messiah to chase out the desecrating Romans.

Jesus failed to fulfill their expectations. And because He didn't fit their job description, they rejected Him. Even faithful and fearless John the Baptist became confused. He dispatched a delegation of disciples to Jesus: "Are You the Coming One, or do we look for another?" (Matthew 11:3). The Baptist also

DESECRATION, DANGER, DELIVERANCE

expected a politically active Messiah to cleanse Jerusalem, and when all Jesus did was teach and heal, John questioned whether He was the real deal.

Similar doubts and delusions overcame the whole nation. This confusion climaxed near the end of Christ's ministry. In John 7 we find Jesus in Jerusalem, attending the Festival of Tabernacles. "There was much complaining among the people concerning Him. Some said, 'He is good'; others said, 'No, on the contrary, He deceives the people'" (verse 12).

The debate about Jesus swept back and forth. Yet another popular misconception of Bible prophecy caused Christ's hearers to question His identity. They whispered: "We know where this Man is from; but when the Christ comes, no one knows where He is from" (verse 27).

Evidently many believed that Messiah would show up suddenly and mysteriously—out of nowhere. Since Jesus had been around awhile, they didn't think He qualified for consideration. Their overall ignorance of prophecy caused them to shun their Savior. It's not that they didn't care about Bible prophecy—they were as excited as our *Left Behind* generation. They just didn't look to the whole scope of Scripture and study it sufficiently for themselves. Sometimes we need to take a second look at the Bible to be sure we understand all that it teaches.

Others in Christ's time knew something of God's Word but still rejected Jesus. Realizing that Messiah would be born in Bethlehem—as Jesus indeed was—they stumbled over the fact that His hometown was Nazareth. "'Will the Christ come out of Galilee? Has not the Scripture said that the Christ comes from the seed of David and from the town of Bethlehem, where David was?' So there was a division among the people because of Him" (verses 41, 43).

A little background check would have resolved their perplexity. Bible prophecy had called for Messiah to live in Nazareth after His birth in Bethlehem (Matthew 2:23). Yet popular misinformation led thousands to reject Jesus.

Follow the Leaders?

False or incomplete information about prophecy can be worse than no information at all. People imagine themselves knowledgeable when they are tragically misinformed.

Do you get the picture? Multitudes in Christ's day got caught up in the popular excitement. Rather than study their Bibles for themselves, they looked to their favorite scribes and spiritual leaders: "Have any of the rulers or the Pharisees believed on Him?" (John 7:48). In other words: "We're not going to follow truth until the religious celebrities we trust lead the way."

Do we hear echoes of that mentality today? Will some Christians not adequately grounded in God's Word unwittingly cooperate with the antichrist's deceptions? A haunting but plausible possibility.

There's too much to lose in earth's last hours to take someone else's word about Bible truth. In the pages of this book, we will study in depth what the Scriptures say about the rapture . . . the tribulation . . . the desecrated temple . . . Armageddon . . . and of course, the antichrist. What we discover may be surprising.

Let's get started by doing a background check on Nicolae Carpathia.

Chapter 2

THE DESECRATION
OF JERUSALEM

Jerusalem was on fire!

Roaring flames spewed orange embers like fire-works into the evening sky. Sizzling coals rained down upon screaming survivors as they fled through smoky streets, soldiers in hot pursuit wielding bloody swords. Buildings collapsed amid the thunder of crashing timbers. Fire as if from hell itself ravaged the Holy City. (Sounds like a preview of the World Trade Center tragedy in New York City.)

The general commanding the attacking forces was the future caesar of Rome. Watching the inferno from a hill outside the city, he saw the fire advancing toward the Temple—the most spectacular building in that part of the world. So amazing was this edifice built by Herod the Great, a client-king of Rome, that the general cringed at the thought of losing it to the flames. So he issued an urgent order: "Don't burn it down!" He wanted it to remain standing as "an ornament" to the empire (Josephus *Wars of the Jews* 6. 4. 3).

But the Jewish Temple was too tempting a target for the rampaging soldiers. After several smaller fires had been ignited and then controlled, one soldier shoved a

12

fiery torch between the hinges of the huge gate. In seconds the cedar-lined inner Temple erupted in flames. Its pinnacles glowed like spikes of red light, the gate towers billowing huge columns of flame and smoke.

Soon the entire Temple Mount blazed like a volcano. Neighboring hillsides and buildings reflected the inferno with an angry orange. Days went by. More carnage followed. Flavius Josephus, Jewish historian who lived through this terrible time, wrote later: "The ground did nowhere appear visible" through the corpses (*ibid.* 6. 5. 1). The Roman troops set more blazes before entering the Temple Court itself, where they offered idolatrous sacrifices and proclaimed Titus "imperator" (*ibid.* 6. 6. 1).

Finally Titus issued orders to burn and sack the entire city (*ibid.* 6. 7. 3), but even this took time to accomplish. Many fled to the subterranean passageways under street level, but to no avail. More conflagrations were set. Days later flames still reached toward the sky over Jerusalem. Residents helplessly watched their holy city burn, some wailing, others vowing vengeance. (Again, this scenario sounds terribly familiar, doesn't it?)

Josephus reports that during the long siege and destruction, 1.1 million people died. Additionally, Roman soldiers captured 97,000 prisoners of war, many of whom were tortured. There is even circumstantial evidence that proceeds from the looting of Jerusalem later helped bankroll the construction of the Colosseum in Rome. (See Louis H. Feldman, "Financing the Colosseum," *Biblical Archaeology Review,* July/August 2001, pp. 20-31, 60, 61.)

A Fate Worse Than Fiction

The preceding scenario happened during the six

DESECRATION, DANGER, DELIVERANCE

long months of April through September in the year
A.D. 70, when Rome sent three legions (somewhere
between 12,000 to 18,000 soldiers) into the area to
quash a Jewish insurrection. (Ten cohorts comprised a
legion, but the actual number of individuals in a co-
hort did not always remain consistent.) Two millennia later, Jews still memorialize the burning of the
Jerusalem Temple each year on the ninth of their
month Ab.

How could this have happened? Didn't God
guarantee protection for Jerusalem, passionately
promising through His prophet: "I will defend this
city, to save it for My own sake and for My servant
David's sake" (Isaiah 37:35)?

God said it, and they believed it. So where was
He now when they needed Him? For many Jews, the
flames ignited by the Romans consumed not just
Jerusalem but also their faith—*misplaced faith in their
city instead of their Messiah, who had walked those streets
just three decades earlier.* Fatal confusion.

You see, in all their confidence about God's blessing on Jerusalem, the unrepentant Jews had not considered a warning from Jesus about their Temple:
"Not one stone shall be left upon another that shall
not be thrown down" (Luke 21:6). A few verses later
He elaborated: "When you see Jerusalem surrounded
by armies, then know that its desolation is near. Then
let those who are in Judea flee to the mountains"
(verses 20, 21).

Jerusalem surrounded by armies? Jesus predicted it
more than 30 years in advance, as a signal for His people to flee before destruction of the city. And so it
happened. In the year A.D. 66 the Roman governor
of Syria, Cestius Gallus, marched south with his army.
Upon arriving at Jerusalem in October, he encoun-

tered Jewish opposition when he marshaled his army outside the city. Rather than pushing forward to storm the city, Cestius unexpectedly and mysteriously withdrew. He just turned his army around and headed north, home to Antioch. Not what you would expect from the mighty Roman army!

But Jesus' followers in Jerusalem took their cue, recognizing God's signal to flee. When the armed forces later returned with overwhelming force to sack Jerusalem, as far as we can determine every last Christian had escaped. Not one who believed and obeyed Christ's warning perished.

It pays to know the truth about Bible predictions—and bring our lives into compliance!

So let's take a closer look at Christ's dramatic and fascinating warning. The Gospels of Matthew and Mark repeat His prophecy about the Temple: "Not one stone shall be left here upon another, that shall not be thrown down" (Matthew 24:2; Mark 13:2). A few verses later Jesus uses intriguing words to refer to what would ultimately happen: " 'The "abomination of desolation," spoken of by Daniel the prophet, [will stand] in the holy place' (whoever reads, let him understand)" (Matthew 24:15; see also Mark 13:14).

So the invasion of Jerusalem and destruction of its Temple would include an "abomination of desolation." This happened as predicted. The Roman troops defiled the Temple Mount by setting up symbols of pagan emperor worship there and within those sacred precincts sacrificing to false gods. Beyond that idolatrous abomination, they also desolated the site with utter destruction. It would have been hard to guess that the Temple had once stood there. Of the entire city complex only three towers that had been part of Herod's own palace, the flat Temple platform, and a portion of the western wall of the city remained intact (*Anchor Bible Dictionary,* vol. 3, p. 761). (One of the towers, called Phasael, still exists as part of the "Tower of David" now seen in modern Jerusalem.)

All this was predicted—decades in advance by Jesus, centuries in advance by Daniel. Just in case anybody missed the importance of Daniel's prophecy, Jesus emphasized: "Let the reader understand."

Might He be speaking to us, also? Perhaps we should explore that ancient prophecy and see what else we might find.

Teenagers Tested

We first need some background about the book of Daniel, one of the most interesting books of all Scripture. Its author is the same one who famously survived the lions' den in Babylon—a story that most of us learned when we were children.

Back when Daniel was just a teenager in Jerusalem, the Hebrew people had become unfaithful and rebellious. Presuming themselves secure in God's covenant with Abraham, they ignored warning after warning. Finally judgment day came when Babylon, headquarters of pagan worship, invaded Jerusalem in 586 B.C. King Nebuchadnezzar besieged and eventually stormed and burned the city. The glorious Temple, built during the reign of King Solomon, King David's son, lay in ruins. (Jewish tradition insists that when the Roman army destroyed the Temple in A.D. 70, it took place on the anniversary day of the Temple destruction caused by Nebuchadnezzar six centuries earlier.) Many Hebrews who survived the attacks were marched in chains to Babylon, a thousand dusty and miserable miles away near the present site of Baghdad, Iraq.

THE DESECRATION OF JERUSALEM

In every time of tribulation God has a faithful few who remain loyal. The opening chapter of the book of Daniel tells how he—Daniel—and three friends stood firm in that heathen city. These four prisoners of war caught the notice of the king and his officials, who found them to be "young men in whom there was no blemish, but good-looking, gifted in all wisdom, possessing knowledge and quick to understand, who had ability to serve in the king's palace, and whom they might teach the language and literature of the Chaldeans" (Daniel 1:4).

Well, those handsome young guys had it made there in Babylon, legendary for its parties and pleasures. No doubt the beautiful young women who lounged around the palace noticed them. At first it must have seemed like the end of the world for Daniel and his friends when the invaders tore them away from their families. But surprise—along came the good life! A scholarship to the University of Babylon and a cushy government job waiting for them upon graduation. With the potential for wine, women, and parties along the way.

"But Daniel purposed in his heart that he would not defile himself with the portion of the king's delicacies, nor with the wine that he drank" (verse 8). Such discipline and integrity served him well through the years as he received promotion after promotion.

Let's pay the aged leader a visit to see how he was doing after all those years. We find him in Daniel 9, the same chapter Jesus referred to regarding Jerusalem's "abomination of desolation." It's quite a prophecy, one of the most exciting in all Scripture. Beyond the bad news about Jerusalem, we also find here good news of Messiah's coming—actually, a calendar countdown to the very year Jesus would launch

His public ministry and then when He would die as our sin offering.

Were you aware that such attestation existed? It's awesome! A prediction more than a half millennium in advance of the *very year* Jesus would begin His ministry.

Calendar Countdown

So let's delve further into Daniel's prophecy. At the beginning of chapter 9, we found Daniel quite concerned. "In the first year of [King Darius'] reign I, Daniel, understood . . . by the word of the Lord, given through Jeremiah the prophet, that He would accomplish seventy years in the desolations of Jerusalem" (verse 2).

So according to prophecy, the Hebrew exiles would remain in Babylonian captivity just 70 years (Jeremiah 25:11, 12). God promised that after this time period expired He would "bring them up and restore them to this place" (Jeremiah 27:22)—"this place" refers to the city of Jerusalem. But something seemed wrong to Daniel. Even though just two years or so remained before those 70 years had fully elapsed, nothing seemed to be happening. Despite his inside government information, he detected nothing in the works preparing the way for the exiles to return to Jerusalem.

Why not? What had happened to God's open-and-shut promise?

Deeply troubled, Daniel brought his perplexity to God. "Then I set my face toward the Lord God to make request by prayer and supplications, with fasting, sackcloth, and ashes" (Daniel 9:3).

Maybe God's promise through Jeremiah was not as open-and-shut a matter as might be assumed. Daniel was aware of another factor involved, something beyond God's willingness to keep His promises.

You see, the exiles had to fulfill their part in the covenant God made with them. All God's covenant promises are conditional upon human allegiance—faith obedience. (See Jeremiah 18:7-10.) When a sovereign in the ancient Near East made a covenant with people, the recipients of the covenant swore a solemn oath of loyalty to that king.

No wonder Daniel was concerned. And notice what he did about it. "And I prayed to the Lord my God, and made confession, and said, 'O Lord, great and awesome God, who keeps His covenant and mercy with those who love Him, and with those who keep His commandments'" (Daniel 9:4). It appears that Daniel had concluded that because of the unfaithfulness of the Hebrew people, the exiles might not get to go back to Jerusalem, even though the duration of their appointed exile had nearly expired. No wonder Daniel was troubled and perplexed.

Suddenly, while he was still praying, Gabriel arrived. (Luke 1:19 identifies Gabriel as an angel from God, as does the Jewish traditional interpretation.) This Messenger now comes with an answer direct from heaven's throne. "O Daniel, I have now come forth to give you skill to understand" (Daniel 9:22).

National Probation

Gabriel proceeded to explain: "Seventy weeks are determined for your people and for your holy city, to finish the transgression, to make an end of sins, to make reconciliation for iniquity, to bring in everlasting righteousness" (verse 24). In other words, God was granting His people a probationary period of 70 weeks to quit trifling with transgression and prepare for their sin-conquering Messiah.

When would this calendar countdown get started?

"From the going forth of the command to restore and build Jerusalem until Messiah the Prince, there shall be seven weeks and sixty-two weeks" (verse 25).

Let's decode this intriguing prophecy about a time span of seven weeks plus 62 weeks, which adds up to 69 weeks. According to the words of this biblical text, the starting point would be a special command to rehabilitate Jerusalem, which, as we have seen, Nebuchadnezzar had destroyed during the Babylonian invasion. These 69 weeks would stretch from the time of that command to restore Jerusalem until Messiah appeared.

Fascinated so far? Let's continue with some quick calculations. Sixty-nine weeks equals a year and a third—specifically *483 days*. Strange, you may say, it was actually more like almost 500 *years* from when Jerusalem was rebuilt until the time of Jesus. And that is correct—*483 years,* to be precise. You see, the word translated *weeks* literally means *sevens*. And this could be regarded as a unit of seven days or a unit of seven years. Watching Daniel 9 in action, it's evident that God gave a time prophecy with 69 units of seven years each, totaling 483 years.

Do you see it? This prophecy foretold that 483 years would separate the time of the command to re-build Jerusalem and the time Messiah would appear. If we know the time when the command to reconstruct Jerusalem was issued, we can calculate forward 483 years and arrive at the time of the Messiah. Or if we know when Jesus Christ—Jesus Messiah (*Christ* is the Greek equivalent of the Hebrew *Messiah*)—appeared, we can work backward in time 483 years and see whether or not an appropriate decree in question was issued then.

THE DESECRATION OF JERUSALEM

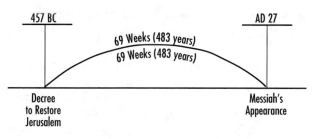

457 BC

AD 27

69 Weeks (483 years)

Decree to Restore Jerusalem

Messiah's Appearance

Jesus Came on Time

Did that really happen? Let's see if we can discover the time when the decree went forth empowering the exiles to restore the city of Jerusalem. No need to guess about that date. The Old Testament records this decree as in the seventh year of the Persian king Artaxerxes, which was 457 B.C. (Ezra 7:11-13). This date is confirmed by modern discoveries in archaeology, a fact recognized by many Bible scholars.

Encyclopedia of Bible Difficulties, a trusted evangelical study source, endorses the year 457 B.C. as the fulfillment of Daniel 9. This book, published by Zondervan, explains how the prophecy unfolds: "If, then, the decree of 457 granted to Ezra himself is taken as the . . . commencement of the . . . 483 years, we come out to the precise year of the appearance of Jesus of Nazareth as Messiah (or Christ): 483 minus 457 comes out to A.D. 26. But since a year is gained in passing from 1 B.C. to A.D. 1 (there being no such year as zero), it actually comes out to A.D. 27. . . . A most remarkable exactitude in the fulfillment of such an ancient prophecy" (Gleason L. Archer, *Encyclopedia of Bible Difficulties,* pp. 290, 291).

So there it is: amazing mathematical documentation that Jesus is the Messiah, which means "anointed one." Jesus became anointed in that role at His baptism, which, to the best of our knowledge, occurred in A.D. 27—the same year foretold by Daniel 9. He then launched His public ministry, announcing: "The time is fulfilled" (Mark 1:15).

What "time" was Jesus talking about? Doesn't it make sense to conclude that He was referring to the prophetic time of Daniel 9—the 69 weeks of years that would introduce "Messiah the Prince"?

Right here is as far as most readers go with the Messianic prophecy of Daniel 9. But, believe it or not, there's more. The most exciting part is yet to come.

Christ's Death
Fulfilled God's Covenant

Back to Jesus, who began His ministry in the year A.D. 27. Soon the religious leaders, jealous of His miracles and influence over the people, determined to kill Him. Again and again they laid plans, but in vain. The Gospel of John records one such episode. "Then they sought to take Him; but no one laid a hand on Him, *because His hour had not yet come*" (John 7:30).

Can we infer from this that there was a specific time set apart for Jesus to die? Yes! And it provides even further dramatic proof that He died for our sins as Messiah. Let's trace this.

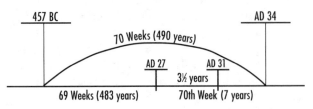

Many, if not most, biblical scholars agree that Christ's public ministry lasted three and a half years. This time period also was foretold in Bible prophecy as a calendar countdown to Calvary. The evening before Jesus died He prayed, "Father, the hour has come" (John 17:1). It was the time foretold by Daniel 9. Notice verse 26: "And after the sixty-two [additional] weeks Messiah shall be cut off, but not for Himself." Obviously here the prophecy describes the sacrifice of Jesus on the cross. He would be "cut off" after the 62 additional weeks (which take us to A.D. 27), but it doesn't say how long afterward.

The next verse does: "Then he shall confirm a covenant with many for one week; but in the middle of the week he shall bring an end to sacrifice and offering. And on the wing of abominations shall be one who makes desolate, even until the consummation, which is determined, is poured out on the desolate" (verse 27). So here we have the cross in the middle of that last week of seven years, which of course is three and a half years after Jesus began His ministry. Sometime after that the abomination of desolation would come.

So, when did Jesus' crucifixion take place? Exactly on schedule! And when He died, the veil inside the Temple sanctuary was torn apart (see Matthew 27:50, 51)—an omen that Jesus, the true sacrifice, had been offered for our sins. The desolation caused by ungodly people would occur when the future Caesar and his Roman army ("the people of the prince" mentioned in Daniel 9:26) invaded Jerusalem with their pagan abominations and destroyed both the city and its Temple.

But before that happened, Jesus confirmed His covenant with the Jewish nation by arriving right on schedule and dying as Messiah precisely in the middle of those final seven years of national opportunity.

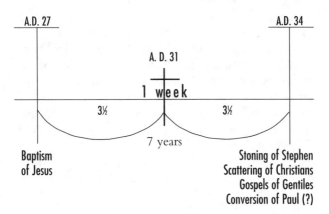

A.D. 27   A.D. 34

A. D. 31

1 week

3½   3½

7 years

Baptism
of Jesus

Stoning of Stephen
Scattering of Christians
Gospels of Gentiles
Conversion of Paul (?)

Accepting Jesus Isn't Optional

Now can you see why, of all the prophecies confirming Jesus as Messiah, Daniel 9 is among the most persuasive and powerful? Because of its mathematical evidence, thousands of Jews have concluded that Jesus is the Jewish Messiah. They know that accepting their Messiah is not something optional, a take-it-or-leave-it matter. Indeed, Jerusalem's future destiny depended upon what it did with its Messiah.

After Calvary God's mercy lingered for His people. This explains why instead of immediately dispatching His disciples across the Roman Empire with the gospel, Jesus sent them first to the "lost sheep of the house of Israel" (Matthew 10:6), "beginning at Jerusalem" (Luke 24:47).

So when Jesus rose from the grave and ascended triumphantly to heaven, He left some additional time for the Jewish nation. But that time was short.

The first Temple burned down in Daniel's day.

The second Temple was destroyed after Christ's day.

THE DESECRATION OF JERUSALEM

Will there be a third temple in Jerusalem in our day? If so, whose temple would it be?

We'll think about that later. But right now as we close this chapter, let's think about *you*. Where do you stand with Jesus? You may know that He is the Messiah of the world, but have you asked Him to become your own Savior?

Taking such a step is as simple as it is profound. We must confess ourselves as sinners before God. We may not imagine we are as bad as those people who get their pictures advertised on the wall at the post office—but we all are sinners in our own way. The Bible says: "All we like sheep have gone astray" (Isaiah 53:6). Nobody's perfect, as the saying goes. Perhaps that's OK according to our thinking, but it can't be OK with God. He is perfect, and we can't measure up to that standard. But He doesn't even want us to try to be good enough to deserve eternal life. That's why Jesus came as our Messiah. "The Lord has laid on Him the iniquity of us all" (verse 6).

Because as sinners we cannot find our way up to God, He came down to us. From Bethlehem He went to Calvary for our sins. But then He rose from the grave and returned to heaven in triumph. Today He takes care of us as our high priest. (We will talk about this, too, in a later chapter.) Soon He will return to take us home with Him to heaven.

Do you want to spend eternity with Jesus and with all your family and friends who also love Him? Then pause right now and tell God that you believe in Him, that you are willing to trust Jesus as your Savior and as the undisputed leader of your life. God will immediately accept you as His child. You may not *feel* different right away, but you belong to God just the same. Believe His promise to accept you, and thank

Him for writing your name in heaven's book of life.

Then what? Like any newborn, you need loving parenting. And so your relationship with God needs to become your top priority—otherwise the devil's distractions will crowd Him out. Take time to talk to Him about everything important to you and to your relationship with Him. That's called "prayer."

And like every newborn, you need nourishment. That's what the Bible is for, as well as books such as this that get you into God's Word. What you learn may be thrilling and instantly fulfilling—or it may confront your favorite habits and longtime beliefs. When that happens just remind yourself who is in control of your life and let Him have His way.

That's how you are saved.

But the antichrist will try to get you lost again. The devil is a lot trickier than most Christians give him credit for. Turn the page if you want to see his deceptions unmasked.

Chapter 3

IN JESUS' NAME— NICOLAE?

Peace be unto you." "Let not your hearts be troubled." "Believe in Me."

Long ago Jesus spoke those soothing words. But not today. You're listening to the blasphemies of Nicolae Carpathia, the *Left Behind* antichrist. He had been killed but then experienced a satanic resurrection. Now he is addressing a huge crowd in New Babylon. They had assembled for his funeral, but suddenly, bursting out of his casket, he came to life before them all.

"You saw me raise myself from the dead," Nicolae reminds the awestruck people. "Who but the most high god has power over death? Who but god controls the earth and sky?"

His voice then affects tenderness as he raises his hands in blessing and entreaty: "Do you still tremble? Fear not, for I bring you good tidings of great joy. It is I who loves you, who stands before you wounded unto death but now living. For you, for you! You need never fear me, for you are my friends. Only my enemies need fear. Why are you fearful, O you of little faith? Come to me and you will find rest for your souls."

DESECRATION, DANGER, DELIVERANCE

David Hassid, a believer and undercover agent for the Tribulation Force in New Babylon, hears all the sacrilege and nearly faints—not from the desert heat but from spiritual nausea. Committed to Jesus, he is not deceived by Nicolae's hostility to the Christian faith and obvious attempt to dethrone Jesus Christ. According to *The Indwelling,* seventh of the *Left Behind* series: "To hear the words of Jesus from this evil man, whom Dr. Ben-Judah taught was now indwelt, satan incarnate, was almost more than he could take."

So David feels sick to his stomach and totally disgusted. But he's not even tempted to be deceived.

Now, picture yourself in that audience, listening to Nicolae Carpathia's swaggering blasphemies. Would you be tricked by someone who demands that you stop worshiping God and worship him instead? Frankly, one would have to be totally ignorant about Christianity to be fooled by anybody who obviously despises the name of Jesus Christ.

Friendly Betrayal

But what if the devil decided to follow a different strategy to entrap believers? Suppose he chooses as his antichrist a trusted Christian leader who pretends to honor Jesus. A wolf in sheep's clothing! Like Judas the betrayer instead of Nicolae the atheist.

Judas was a prototype of the antichrist. Was he openly hostile to Christ? No; he was a respected and apparently respectable disciple. The strategy was so successful that his fellow disciples suspected nothing, not even on the night he betrayed Jesus. Now, if Judas had cursed Christ and built an idolatrous image of himself in Jerusalem, demanding worship, would the disciples have been thus fooled? Disgusted, yes. But not deceived.

IN JESUS' NAME—NICOLAE?

Jesus warned that in the last days the devil would be so cunning as to "deceive, if possible, even the elect" (Matthew 24:24). Hidden hostility is always more deceptive than a frontal assault. So Nicolae would have been smarter to betray the Tribulation Force with a kiss instead of attacking it with fire-breathing threats.

The supreme deception would be that by following his teachings you would be obeying at least some biblical truth. Remember, Christ said: "If you love Me, keep My commandments" (John 14:15). Now, what if the antichrist power substituted some of its own commandments among God's commandments and thus stole your obedience and loyalty? All of it in the name of Jesus! *That* would be deceptive, wouldn't you say?

Christian Face of the Antichrist

You may be thinking, *I can see that an antichrist like Judas would be much more deceptive for believers than Nicolae. But isn't the antichrist supposed to attack Christianity openly?*

Not necessarily. Let's get some background on the word "antichrist." The Greek word translated "anti" in the word *"anti*christ" can mean either "against" or "instead of." So the antichrist power by definition is not necessarily some obvious enemy of Christianity. Instead, the antichrist might assume titles and roles that belong exclusively to Jesus, all the while giving Him lip service. This would be the wolf in sheep's clothing that Jesus warned about in Matthew 7:15. Or like a spy planted inside the CIA, proclaiming loyalty to America while secretly betraying it to the enemy. Stealth and infiltration is much more deceptive and dangerous than outright hostility.

So, then, the devil has two possible options for his antichrist: the hateful Nicolae or a betraying Judas-style church leadership. We don't need to guess which route the enemy will take. Jesus warned: "Take heed that no one deceives you" (Matthew 24:4). And did you notice exactly whom he hopes to deceive? *You*—a believer! *The purpose of the antichrist is to deceive the saints. The devil already has everybody else.*

Jesus Gets Left Behind

Our last chapter unfolded the thrilling calendar countdown, found in Daniel 9, to Christ's ministry. As you recall, it predicted the year of His baptism and the year of His death as the climax of Messiah's confirmation of the covenant. But somehow many sincere Christians take this convincing prophecy about the work of Christ and substitute in His place the work of the antichrist. They actually remove Jesus from part of Daniel 9, replacing Him with the antichrist!

Here's how. They take the last seven years (the seventieth week of years) and disconnect them from the other 69 weeks. Nothing in the text calls for this. Nevertheless, they take that last week of seven years (the seventieth week) and push it way off into the future. Then they call the 2,000-year gap that they have created the "church age."

So the gap, or parenthesis, that they insert between the sixty-ninth and seventieth weeks of Daniel, is of human devising—well intentioned, no doubt, but still mistaken. Worse yet, some scholars and authors take the death of Jesus that Daniel 9 foretold would occur in the middle of those seven years (the seventieth week) and substitute the death of the antichrist after the rapture.

IN JESUS' NAME—NICOLAE?

Is this not a serious spiritual deception?

We have here one of the most perplexing aspects of the *Left Behind* prophetic scenario. Despite the obvious sincerity of the authors, when they put the death of Nicolae where the death of Jesus belongs, our Lord Himself gets left behind!

God's Covenant, Not Nicolae's

There's yet another concern we must notice. Daniel 9 is all about the covenant between God and His people. (See verse 4.) Jesus appears as Messiah after the sixty-ninth week for the purpose of confirming that salvation covenant. His death in the midst of that seventieth week is the very heart of its fulfillment, and our only hope as well. When He died, the sanctuary veil was torn in two, symbolizing the ultimate end of the significance of Jewish Temple services. By His once-for-all-time sacrifice for sin, Jesus confirmed God's covenant promise to "bring an end to sacrifice and offering" (verse 27).

But somehow *Left Behind* takes Christ's covenant and calls it the antichrist's covenant. You may find it surprising that Scripture never teaches that the antichrist power will either make or break any kind of covenant with anybody. The covenant of Daniel 9 belongs to Christ. To give it instead to the antichrist—is that not doing the very work of the antichrist himself?

There's a real problem here, we must admit—made all the more treacherous by the genuine Christian faith and zeal of its proponents. Our next chapter will explore the medieval roots of this confusion, but first let's get deeper into what the New Testament says about the antichrist.

Seven Identifiers
of the Antichrist

"Let no one deceive you by any means; for that Day will not come unless the falling away comes first, and the man of sin is revealed, the son of perdition, who opposes and exalts himself above all that is called God or that is worshiped, so that he sits as God in the temple of God, showing himself that he is God" (2 Thessalonians 2:3, 4). Christians everywhere understand this "man of sin" to symbolize the antichrist power. Paul "does not use the term Antichrist, but it is Antichrist that he has in mind" (Leon Morris, *Tyndale New Testament Commentaries,* 1 and 2 Thessalonians, vol. 13, p. 127). We find in this passage seven key identifiers.

1. Once again we find a warning against deception. The devil knows he can't stop Jesus from returning, so he spreads his deceptions to confuse sincere believers who are excited about Bible prophecy.

2. The antichrist doesn't set up a counterfeit anti-Christian temple, as the imaginary character Nicolae Carpathia does. The real antichrist operates *in the temple of God*. Not a temple *like* God's, but actually in God's own temple.

You may wonder where this temple is and when it will be built.

3. Actually, God's temple on earth is not a real building of any kind—it's His people, the body of Christ. Paul told the Christian church that as a community of believers, *"You* are God's building. . . . *You* are the temple of God" (1 Corinthians 3:9-16). So the temple of God in which the antichrist works is the Christian church. Again it makes sense, based on the biblical evidence, to envision the antichrist as Judas-type Christian leadership operating from within the church.

The next key identifier confirms this assumption.

4. The antichrist emerges from a "falling away." The New Testament Greek word here is *apostasia,* which in secular Greek referred to military or political rebellion and came also to refer to a falling away from truth. We use the word today when we speak of "apostasy." Since the "church of the living God" is "the pillar and ground of the truth" (1 Timothy 3:15), this represents a backsliding from truth inside the church—not an attack from outside Christianity, such as from the fictional Carpathia. The apostle Paul predicted this in a speech to church leaders: *"From among yourselves men will rise up, speaking perverse things, to draw away the disciples after themselves"* (Acts 20:30).

What type of "perverse things"? We get a clue from the word "sin" in the expression "man of sin." It means lawlessness. So the antichrist church leadership will undermine God's commandments with false teachings of its own that masquerade as genuine Bible truth.

The next point is huge.

5. The anti-Christian power will emerge within the church *before* the rapture! How do we know? The passage we're looking at speaks of "that Day." And which day is this? Look at verse 1: the day of "the coming of our Lord Jesus Christ and our gathering together to Him." "Our" refers to the saints, the church, to whom Paul is addressing his Epistle (2 Thessalonians 1:1). So "our gathering together to Christ" is the rapture of the church—and the Bible says that this won't happen until *after* the working of antichrist.

God knew His people would get confused about this particular point. Long ago He anticipated there would be a theory that the antichrist would not come until after the rapture. And so He warns specifically on this point: "Let no one deceive you by *any means*"—that certainly would include sermons, books, and movies.

So then, the antichrist arrives *before* the rapture. Do we know how long before?

6. Paul makes a stunning revelation regarding the antichrist power: "The mystery of lawlessness is *already at work*" (verse 7). Already in the first century the seeds of apostasy existed. Even as the New Testament was written, the antichrist power was secretly working within the church, causing truth decay. We saw how Paul warned about this, and so did the apostle Peter: "There will be false teachers among you, who will secretly bring in destructive heresies" (2 Peter 2:1).

Let's trace this further by examining the term *"mystery* of lawlessness." It is not easy to understand completely what the word meant, but it seems safe to say that it typically referred to something that was hidden or kept secret. Marvin R. Vincent, in his well-known book series titled *Word Studies in the New Testament,* published by William B. Eerdmans, wrote: "A mystery does not lie in the obscurity of a thing, but in its secrecy" (vol. 4, p. 64). It suggests to me a conspiracy of some sort.

Evidently the antichrist involves a conspiracy, and a conspiracy, by its very definition, has to involve more than a single person. It appears to be a group of Christian leaders or a succession of leaders who, working over time, cause a gradual "falling away" from truth in undermining God's commandments. The antichrist mystery develops throughout the long centuries until making a final, personal expression just before Christ's coming.

We see this in our final key identifier.

7. The return of Jesus to gather His church will destroy the antichrist power: "And then the lawless one will be revealed, whom the Lord will consume

with the breath of His mouth and destroy with the brightness of His coming. The coming of the lawless one is according to the working of Satan, with all power, signs, and lying wonders, and with all unrighteous deception among those who perish, because they did not receive the love of the truth, that they might be saved" (2 Thessalonians 2:8-10).

Evangelical biblical scholar Leon Morris notes: "It is as though Satan were throwing all his forces into one last despairing effort" (*Tyndale New Testament Commentaries,* 1 and 2 Thessalonians, vol. 13, p. 126).

So immediately before the rapture will come the ultimate expression of the antichrist—a satanic miracle worker. However, *unlike Nicolae Carpathia, this personage will not oppose Christ but masquerade as Him.* Did you notice that word "deception" again? Instead of denying or attacking Christianity, the antichrist will sabotage the faith with "lying wonders"—spectacular miracles in the name of Jesus. He will not denounce the Bible but rather misinterpret its teachings so as to promote lawlessness— some cleverly contrived violation of God's law, the Ten Commandments.

The antichrist's lies will multiply until a final satanic manifestation will meet destruction at the second coming of Jesus—"our gathering together unto Him"—the rapture of the saints. We'll explore the rapture itself in chapter 5.

It's Not About Politics

Meanwhile, remember that the antichrist will be not a political leader but a religious deceiver. He will not care about your political loyalties. He wants your soul. And he will find success in deceiving all those who would rather be entertained with miracles or spiritual fiction than "receive the love of the truth, that they might be saved."

All the time we have been scouting the horizon for Nicolae, the deceptions of the antichrist have slithered in unnoticed, welcomed into the church. Perhaps the truth on this subject has startled you. Maybe your head is spinning from all you've seen in this chapter. Relax. Things will get sorted out as we continue.

Just keep your mind open—and your Bible close by.

Chapter 4

NICOLAE'S FAMILY TREE

I am the god above all other gods. There is none like me. Worship or beware."

It's Nicolae Carpathia again. The huge New Babylon crowd gasps at his bold claims.

False prophet Leon Fortunato further terrifies the crowd with his own threat: "Marvel not that I say unto you, some shall surely die. If Carpathia is not god, and I am not his chosen one, then I shall be proved wrong. If Carpathia is not THE only way and THE only life, then what I say is not THE only truth, and none should fear."

Fortunato becomes even bolder in his blasphemy: "I now call upon the power of my most high god to prove that he rules from heaven by burning to death with his pure extinguishing fire those who would oppose me—those who would deny his deity, those who would subvert and plot and scheme to take my rightful place as his spokesman."

After a dramatic pause, the false prophet concludes: "I pray he does this even as I speak."

Leon Fortunato turns to face Carpathia's 10 regional potentates and points at three who oppose him.

Beams of fire burst from the cloudless sky and incinerate the three where they sit. The other seven leap from their seats to avoid the heat and the flames. The crowd shrieks and wails, but no one dares to flee. Every soul seems paralyzed by fear. Meanwhile, the fire that leaves three tiny smoldering piles of ash disappears as suddenly as it had come.

This is the *Left Behind* scenario of the antichrist and his image. Is it scriptural? Interestingly, the Protestant Reformers had a much different concept of the antichrist and his 10 regional powers, three of whom were destroyed.

Medieval Roots

Life was bleak in 1517 medieval Germany. Suddenly a little excitement came to the town of Jüterbog. Dominican monk Johann Tetzel showed up with salvation for sale. With bells pealing and children shouting, he paraded through the gates and planted his colorful banner in the town square. Tetzel held the exclusive regional franchise for selling "indulgences," which supposedly provided the purchaser fire insurance against future punishment in purgatory, plus release for souls already suffering there.

Actually, of the money he raised, about half went directly to Pope Leo X to help rebuild St. Peter's Basilica in Rome, and the rest ended up in the hands of twenty-something Margrave Albert of Brandenburg, who had recently paid dearly (20,000 florins) for his new positions as archbishop of Mainz and Magdeburg and bishop of Halberstadt.

Tetzel displayed his authorization from church headquarters for all to see, framed upon a background of red and gold velvet. Then he got down to business. The carnival spirit waned somewhat as he launched into a spine-chilling description of souls writhing in purgatory. Finally, pointing to the stack of indulgences beside him, he closed his sales pitch: "As soon as the coin in the coffer rings, the soul from purgatory springs."

Tetzel's poetic flair wasn't Billy Graham's style, yet many came forward and purchased pardons. Tetzel had been banned from selling his "jubilee indulgences" in the town of Wittenberg, where Martin Luther preached, but some of Luther's parishioners trekked to nearby Jüterbog and then came back, waving their newly purchased indulgences.

He vowed: "I'll knock a hole in his drum." He did that and much more, and the world has never been the same.

First, Luther preached mightily against selling such pardons. Next, he seized his pen and composed—in Latin—a powerful series of objections to the peddling of jubilee indulgences. On Halloween of 1517 he grabbed a hammer and nailed those ninety-five theses to the heavy wooden door of Wittenberg's cathedral. They reflected Luther's trademark style—courageous, concise, compelling.

"Saints have no extra credits," he thundered. "And Christ's merits are freely available. . . . If the pope does have power to release anyone from purgatory, why in the name of love does he not abolish purgatory by letting everyone out?"

Luther defied anyone to debate him. Copies of his theses multiplied throughout Europe. Rome ultimately pronounced him a rebel and heretic, warning him to recant or face church punishment. Instead, the Reformer pressed forward. He acclaimed Jesus as the only true mediator for sinners, accusing the church of interfering with a believer's personal relationship with God.

Catholic scholars today agree that the church in

Luther's time was ripe for reform. Politics had displaced piety. Spiritual confusion abounded. Not long before, three rival church leaders at the same time had claimed to be pope, with each condemning the others as being the dreaded antichrist. Luther wryly remarked that they all had been correct—and suggested that the church system itself had become the antichrist power.

Not surprisingly, the Reformer's stand alienated him from Rome. The divorce became final when Luther officially condemned the papal power as antichrist. Pope Leo X returned the favor with a declaration of excommunication on January 3, 1521, though Luther himself never intended to leave his beloved church. After all, he was an Augustinian monk. The pope banned Luther's writings, ordering them to be burned..

Was Luther hyperventilating in the heat of battle when he declared that the church had become the antichrist's headquarters?

It would not be fair to blame the church today for its sins of yesterday, of course. As we will see in later chapters, the Reformers themselves, despite their insights, frequently failed to reflect the spirit of Jesus. Many Protestants today are unaware that the Reformers often persecuted those they considered heretics, both Roman Catholics and even fellow Protestants. Our purpose here is not to point fingers at our ancestors, Catholic or Protestant, but to understand how the various Bible passages about the antichrist were interpreted in Reformation times. Perhaps we can learn lessons from history and gain background for our own study.

What stands out is that the Reformers located the antichrist within Christianity itself. They did this based upon careful study of those passages we looked at in our previous chapter. They observed that the antichrist

- emerges out of an apostasy, that is, a falling away from truth.
- takes Christ's name while undermining His truth.
- operates within the church leadership structure, as did Judas.
- may function as a person or a power.
- had roots in early Christian history.
- is destroyed by Christ's second coming.

Subtle Opposition

Let's probe deeper into church history and see how the Christian church went astray by adopting anti-Christian beliefs. Recall that the apostle Peter warned the New Testament believers: "There will be false teachers among you, who will secretly bring in destructive heresies" (2 Peter 2:1). This happened exactly as predicted. Should this surprise us? After all, had not God's people throughout Old Testament history continually wandered from the covenant?

Apostasy in the post-New Testament era appears to have been far more subtle than it had been in Old Testament times. Pagan ceremonies and holy days infiltrated the church and soon became enshrined as Christian traditions. The absorption of these practices into the Christian church may have been prompted by relatively innocent motives, but the consequences that followed did not honor biblical truth. Many of the same believers who stood firmly against persecution allowed pagan influences to taint their faith. Church leadership compromised the gospel, and Christianity in general suffered a serious loss of faith. This anti-Christian process claimed to honor Christ even while subverting His authority.

For example, the Bible says that there is just "one

Mediator between God and men, the Man Christ Jesus" (1 Timothy 2:5). The church, however, exalted its saints as mediators, putting them where Christ alone belongs—the very work of antichrist, whereby Christ in His unique role was replaced by mere humans.

The church also acclaimed Mary as "Queen of Heaven," whereas the Bible bestows no such honor upon her, giving all celestial glory to God alone.

And then there is the concept of a purgatory for imperfect believers, which denies the truth that "there is therefore now no condemnation to those who are in Christ Jesus" (Romans 8:1).

All these teachings of the church, and others, seriously subvert Christian faith even while professing to uphold it. This anti-Christian "falling away" from gospel truth is regrettable and inexcusable, yet it is just what the New Testament had predicted.

Daniel's Ancient Prophecy

We turn now to an Old Testament prophecy that convinced the Reformers about the antichrist. Daniel 7 records the fascinating prediction. It's a prophecy concerning four beasts, or kingdoms. Verse 23 explains that "the fourth beast shall be a fourth kingdom on earth, which shall be different from all other kingdoms."

Many Bible scholars agree that the four kingdoms of Daniel 7 are Babylon, Greece, Persia, and Rome. According to this text, the fourth kingdom, the Roman Empire, would be different from the other three. At first—in A.D. 395—the Roman Empire was split into two parts, the Western and the Eastern prefectures. Then in A.D. 476, rather than giving way to another single power, the Western prefecture was pulled apart as a result of the inroads made by 10 "barbarian" kingdoms. Notice: "The ten horns are ten kings who shall arise from this kingdom. And another shall rise after them; he shall be different from the first ones, and shall subdue three kings" (verse 24).

The fact is that modern Europe has descended from 10 Germanic tribes that invaded and helped dissect the Western Roman Empire. (The Eastern Roman Empire, also called the Byzantine Empire, outlasted the western half of the empire, lasting for 11 centuries and finally succumbing in A.D. 1453, when the Turks captured Constantinople.)

And our text prophesied that three of those tribes would succumb to a new power, also headquartered in Rome—a religious and political coalition that eventually developed into the Holy Roman Empire. It's intriguing to consider how this happened.

In the early fourth century the Roman Empire was sagging with age. Threats loomed both within and beyond its borders. Confronted with steady problems, the emperor Constantine converted to Christianity—a remarkable development, given the hostility of previous emperors toward the church. Constantine quickly launched a campaign to Christianize his kingdom.

Problems persisted, however. Seeking escape from economic headaches and the threat of invasion from barbarian tribes, the emperor relocated 800 miles east of Rome. Constantinople (now Istanbul, Turkey) became his capital. From this time forward, the Roman Church dominated the western half of the empire.

So history confirms the prediction that a religious power in Rome would succeed its secular leadership. A popular college textbook certifies this transfer of power from the Roman Empire to the Roman Church: "In the West, the church took over the defense of Roman civilization. The emperor gave up the [pagan] title of Pontifex Maximus (high priest) because the Roman gods were no longer worshiped. The bishop of Rome assumed these priestly functions, and this is why the Pope today is sometimes referred to as the Pontiff. . . . The Roman Empire had become the Christian Church" (Harry A. Dawe, *Ancient Greece and Rome: World Cultures in Perspective,* p. 188).

World Book Encyclopedia agrees: "The Roman Empire transmitted its social and economic system to the Middle Ages. . . . During the Middle Ages the Roman Catholic Church replaced the Roman Empire as the unifying force in Europe" (vol. 16, p. 448).

What happened? When the Huns, a fierce tribe led by brutal Attila, swept into Italy and threatened to destroy Rome, Pope Leo—not the emperor—met the barbarian. Attila was so impressed with the pontiff's spiritual power that he turned back. What Leo said to Attila remains unknown, but what is significant is the fact that it was the pope and not the emperor who guarded the gates of Rome.

Rome eventually fell to the barbarian tribes—10 of them, just as Daniel 7 had predicted a millennium beforehand. The church, however, managed to convert the invaders, thus maintaining its control of the Western Empire. What about those three tribes that resisted Rome's authority?

In A.D. 533 Emperor Justinian officially declared the Roman pontiff to be "head of all the holy churches." In harmony with this declaration he waged war on anyone who refused to honor the authority of the church. Three of the tribes—the Herulis, the Ostrogoths, and the Vandals—refused to submit to the Papacy. But in March of 538 the last of those rebel tribes fell, and the pontiff reigned supreme over Western Christendom.

So 10 kingdoms followed Western Rome, and three of them fell to make way for the Papacy. Is this just a coincidence, or a striking fulfillment of the prophecy that he "shall subdue three kings" (Daniel 7:24)?

We will return to this and probe deeper in chapter 9. Let's return to the time of the Reformation.

The Catholic Reformation

Back in the sixteenth century the Protestant Reformation was followed by a reformation in the Catholic Church. The pope at that time, concerned about suffering staggering losses to the Protestants, summoned church leaders to the northern Italian city of Trent to consider corrective measures. At this Council of Trent, Catholics finally and forcefully addressed many of the abuses and excesses that Luther and others had challenged and condemned. But rather than bring their basic beliefs into line with Scripture, they reaffirmed church tradition as a legitimate basis of doctrine and laid plans to enforce it. Through political maneuvering—and the Inquisition—papal Rome regained large territories lost to the Protestants.

The Jesuits, a new religious order, implemented the Catholic Reformation. They trained tirelessly and served sacrificially in their assignment of counteracting the Protestant Reformation. Along with a remarkable missionary outreach, the Jesuits devoted themselves to education and research. Two of their best scholars, Luis de Alcazar and Francisco Ribera, confronted the most explosive charge of the Protestants—that the church had become the antichrist.

Alcazar suggested that the prophecies regarding antichrist had been fulfilled in the past with the pagan Roman Empire, before the popes gained power. His position became known among biblical scholars as *preterism*. Ribera, following the lead of some of the "church fathers," taught the opposite view, *futurism*. He interpreted the biblical evidence to support the idea that the antichrist would arise in power only in the last days. Either way, whether the antichrist was past or future, the Jesuits had achieved their goal. They had taken the heat off the pope.

How did Ribera manage to relegate into the far-off future the prophecies concerning the antichrist? By reinterpreting the prophecy of Daniel 9, which fore-told the year of Christ's death. Ribera replaced Christ with the antichrist there, thus laying the foundation for the *Left Behind* prophetic scenario, as we shall see.

Predictably, Protestant leaders rejected Roman Catholic futurism. Of two dozen major Reformation scholars between 1639 and the end of the seventeenth century, every one still referred to the antichrist as the established Roman Church and that Jesus had fulfilled the 70-weeks prophecy of Daniel.

But amazingly, Protestants in the past two centuries have abandoned the prophetic faith of their founders by adopting and adapting the futurism of the Jesuits. Of all the surprises in the development of Christian teaching, what can surpass this?

George Eldon Ladd, an honored evangelical scholar of our day, documents it. "It will probably come as a shock to many modern futurists to be told that the first scholar in relatively modern times who returned to the patristic futuristic interpretation was a Spanish Jesuit named Ribera. In 1590 Ribera pub-lished a commentary on the Revelation as a counter-interpretation to the prevailing view among Protestants which identified the Papacy with the Antichrist. Ribera applied all of Revelation but the earliest chapters to the end time rather than to the history of the Church. Antichrist would be a single evil person who would be received by the Jews and would rebuild Jerusalem, abolish Christianity, deny Christ, persecute the Church and rule the world for three and a half years" (*The Blessed Hope,* pp. 37, 38).

Autopsy of Apostasy

So Protestants have suffered a serious loss of their prophetic heritage. How did they come to accept Jesuit interpretations over those of the Reformers— the founders of their faith?

We must go back to the early 1830s. Edward Irving, an influential pastor within the Church of Scotland, became fascinated by the predictions of Christ's second coming and cofounded the Society for the Investigation of Prophecy. Unfortunately, he accepted Ribera's futurism and even translated the book of a Spanish Jesuit scholar.

Irving captured the interest of London's high society as well as the populace. In Scotland he taught an outdoor audience of some 12,000 people. Although Irving died in middle age, his influence survived and thrived. Through his teaching, Irish Anglican John Nelson Darby adopted Ribera's futurism. This zealous and pious young man journeyed around Europe and the United States, proclaiming his beliefs. When he died in 1882 Darby could number nearly 100 study groups in America committed to his prophetic interpretations.

After Darby, the torch of futurism passed to C. I. Scofield, compiler of the study notes in the *Scofield Reference Bible*. First published in 1909, Scofield's Bible remains popular today. Since 1970 Hal Lindsey's best-seller *The Late Great Planet Earth* has influenced millions of Protestants to accept a futurist view of the antichrist. And now we have the *Left Behind* series.

So, what do we make of all this? The incredible yet inescapable conclusion is that many Protestants today base their prophetic interpretations on an old diversionary teaching of Rome's warfare against the Protestant Reformation. No wonder so much confusion exists today about this loss of prophetic faith.

Not all, of course, have been so deceived. Just recently one evangelical (and strongly Calvinistic) publication printed a review of these popular books about last-day events and the rapture. The author refers to these publications as part of "the plethora of speculative prophetic literature," but it is all "the same old stuff" that tries to make "contemporary current events . . . correlate with the . . . Dispensational interpretation of Scripture" (*Searching Together,* Spring 2001, p. 9). The reviewer insists that these attempts fly in the face of important biblical truths and principles. "Yet people continue to waste large amounts of their money on such writings, as the *Left Behind* series shows" (*ibid.,* p. 11).

Those who cherish the heritage of the Reformation may well feel concerned. Yet many others simply shrug their shoulders and say: "What difference does it make what we believe about the antichrist, so long as we sincerely believe in the real Christ?"

Well, if we really are sincere about Jesus, will we not take His Word seriously with its warnings about prophetic deceptions? Will we not brush aside all error and insist upon pure truth?

There's too much to lose in earth's last hours to take someone else's word about what the Bible supposedly says. God can help us study the Scriptures for ourselves. It is time to move forward in obedience to His sure word of prophecy.

Chapter 5

LEFT BEHIND DEAD

It happened the moment they kissed.

In the movie, that is. The instant Captain Rayford Steele shared a stolen kiss with Hattie Durham, the rapture occurred. People on the Europe-bound airliner vanished, slipping invisibly into the night sky. Pandemonium broke out among those left behind. Back home Rayford's wife, Irene, and their young son disappeared, leaving him and Chloe lonely and grieving.

Christians everywhere rejoice that they will not be left behind like that when Jesus returns for His saints. Bumper stickers proclaim: "If I'm Raptured, Take the Wheel" and "Warning: Driver Will Be Raptured Any Moment."

It's intriguing to imagine what it would be like to vanish suddenly and silently and meet the Lord. But is this what the Bible teaches?

Secret of the Rapture

First, we find that the word "rapture" itself is not in most English Bibles. It comes from a Latin word meaning "to snatch or carry away." The Greek New Testament equivalent for "rapture" shows up in the Latin version of 1 Thessalonians 4:16, 17: "For the

Lord Himself will descend from heaven with a shout, with the voice of an archangel, and with the trumpet of God. And the dead in Christ will rise first. Then we who are alive and remain shall be caught up together [raptured] with them in the clouds to meet the Lord in the air. And thus we shall always be with the Lord."

Christ's coming will be the most audible and visible, spectacular event of all time! Jesus appears from heaven, bursting through the clouds with a shout of joy to rescue His saints. The lead angel in Christ's victory procession shouts as well. Then there's a mighty blast from God's trumpet. Nothing secret about this at all.

According to the *Left Behind* series, Christ's glorious coming is not for the church but for those who had been left behind from a previous coming—the so-called rapture. But the passage we read is specifically addressed to the church (verse 1), and Paul uses the words "we" in connection with Christ's coming. Obviously this vocal and visible event is intended for the church.

Christ Describes His Coming

Jesus predicted that everyone on earth will know when He returns to gather His elect saints. "Then the sign of the Son of Man will appear in heaven, and then all the tribes of the earth will mourn, and they will see the Son of Man coming on the clouds of heaven with power and great glory. And He will send His angels with a great sound of a trumpet, and they will gather together His elect" (Matthew 24:30, 31).

It is true that the Bible says that Christ will come unexpectedly, like a thief in the night. But does this mean the world won't realize when it's happening?

Much as we may wish we could, it is impossible to forget the awful morning of September 11, 2001, when from the clear blue sky terrorists struck

America. Though intelligence agencies for years had warned about a domestic attack from Islamic militants, the sudden strike caught everyone (including the government) by surprise. But once it happened, everyone knew about it. So it will be at the return of Jesus. Despite worldwide warnings, the unsaved engaged in business as usual will be caught by surprise, but they certainly will be aware of Christ's appearing.

What happens to those unready to meet Jesus? Will they have a second chance to repent? Again, let's see what Jesus taught. "And as it was in the days of Noah, so it will be also in the days of the Son of Man: They ate, they drank, they married wives, they were given in marriage, until the day that Noah entered the ark, and the flood came and *destroyed them all*" (Luke 17:26, 27).

Christ's coming for His elect will bring total destruction to this earth and its inhabitants, just as in the days of Noah. The world then, as now, was engrossed in business as usual until God's final, fatal surprise. All who neglected heaven's warning perished on the spot. "Even so will it be in the day when the Son of Man is revealed" (verse 30).

After Christ's coming, the bodies of the lost lie scattered across the earth. Those left behind are all dead: "Two people will be in one bed; one will be taken and the other left. Two women will be grinding grain together; one will be taken and the other left. 'Where Lord?' they asked. He replied 'Where there is a *dead body,* there the vultures will gather'" (Luke 17:34-37, NIV).

So there is no second chance. Nothing in Scripture says that anybody—Jew or Gentile—can be saved after Jesus returns. This is one of the most regrettable fictions of the *Left Behind* series. It offers fatally false hope for sinners who don't want to repent now because they're having too much fun in Las Vegas. Of course the authors of *Left Behind* urge everybody to come to Jesus now, but many prodigals are natural risk-takers. They *like* living dangerously. For them, the challenge of playing international cat and mouse with Nicolae offers radical adventure and romance. They want to get in on the action with Chloe and Buck. They want to ride the helicopter with Albie and Rayford. Besides, these Trib Force guys and their women seem much more exciting and glamorous than the sleepy churchgoers next door.

So why not put off repentance until after the rapture? You win both ways: First, you get to party as you please now when religion seems a drag; later, when all the boring believers disappear, you take your clue to switch sides. You can join up with God's SWAT team and then become an instant hero, according to the *Left Behind* scenario.

Deadly delusion! If you care to base your faith on the Bible rather than religious fiction, please note that human probation ends at the coming of Jesus for His church. So Bruce and Rayford and everybody else would have been destroyed by the brightness of Christ's coming—even Tsion—for having putting off their preparation. Yes, there will be a tribulation—complete with antichrist—but it all happens *before* Christ's coming. So if you want to be on God's team, you need to get on board *now*.

Jesus Isn't Sneaky

Well, how did a dangerous falsehood like the secret rapture get started? It's rooted in a medieval myth recently popularized among Protestants, which we noticed in chapter 3. If you recall, we saw there that the rapture of the church, according to Scripture, happens *after* the antichrist is revealed, who then is destroyed with the glory of Christ's coming for His church.

Think about it. Why would Jesus want to sneak us up to heaven? He's waited 2,000 years to come and get His church. Why shouldn't that be a triumphant event, full of celestial celebration? And so His second coming will be the most magnificent event in human history—and everyone will know about it.

But wait a minute. Doesn't the Bible teach that Jesus will come in the "twinkling of an eye"? No. What it says is that the resurrected saints will be *changed* in a moment, in the twinkling of an eye: "We shall not all sleep, but we shall all be *changed—in a moment,* in the twinkling of an eye, at the last trumpet. For the trumpet will sound, and the dead will be raised incorruptible, and we shall be changed. For this corruptible must put on incorruption, and this mortal must put on immortality, then shall be brought to pass the saying that is written: 'Death is swallowed up in victory'" (1 Corinthians 15:51-54).

So those who are asleep—that is, deceased believers—get resurrected when Jesus returns. (Did you notice those trumpets again? Apparently the "twinkling of an eye" transformation is anything but silent.) Then the living saints are changed instantly, swapping these worn-out, sinful bodies doomed to death for eternally youthful bodies of perfection. I won't mind that, will you?

What happens next after we all meet the Lord in the air? Remember that well-known promise of Jesus? "Let not your heart be troubled; you believe in God, believe also in Me. In My Father's house are many mansions. . . . I go to prepare a place for you. And if I go and prepare a place for you, I will come again and receive you to Myself; that where I am, there you may be also (John 14:1-3).

A space trip to heaven through the stars! And quite a welcome is waiting. God Himself greets us. Angels crowd around us. We'll enjoy a homecoming banquet better than any Thanksgiving dinner on earth. (See Matthew 8:11; Luke 12:37.)

Reigning in Heaven

After we settle into our heavenly home, we will live as royalty up there. "Blessed and holy is the one who has a part in the first resurrection; over these the second death has no power, but they will be priests of God and of Christ and will reign with Him for a thousand years" (Revelation 20:6, NASB).

The first resurrection, the raising of believers when Jesus comes, marks the beginning of this millennium. Only afterward comes the resurrection of those who rejected Jesus. "The rest of the dead did not come to life until the thousand years were completed" (verse 5, NASB). The unsaved are resurrected to face God's white throne of judgment and the second death. But this will not happen until all living beings in the universe fully understand why they must be lost—and you and I will participate in that evaluation. So the apostle Paul speaks of a time when "the saints will judge the world" (1 Corinthians 6:2). This part of the judgment happens during our millennium in heaven while reigning with Jesus. "And I saw thrones, and they sat on them, and judgment was committed to them" (Revelation 20:4).

God will open to us the books of record, and we'll have plenty of time to ask all our questions. Down here life often makes no sense, even though all the while God is working everything out for our good. Jesus said everything hidden on earth now will be revealed in the future (Luke 12:2). At last in heaven we will fully comprehend whatever in this life we must accept only by faith.

Important questions will get answers, and our curious questions too about the hidden things of history. Secrets of the White House, the Kremlin, and the Mafia. Secrets of the pharaohs, Caesars, and popes.

Attack on the New Jerusalem

After the millennium in heaven, God once again turns His attention to earth. Ever since the brightness of the rapture destroyed the antichrist and his followers (2 Thessalonians 2:8), this earth has been desolate and depopulated (Jeremiah 4:23-27). Only the devil and his angels are down here with nothing to do but ponder the misery they caused. Before Christ's coming, Satan had been going around like a roaring lion to deceive and devour people, but now he is chained by circumstances with nobody to tempt—the saints are in heaven and the unsaved are still dead, awaiting their final judgment.

Following the thousand years comes the resurrection of the wicked. Suddenly Satan has his people back, which frees him from his millennial exile. He moves quickly to rally his resurrected rebels. The book of Revelation records the drama. "And they came up on the broad plain of the earth and surrounded the camp of the saints and the beloved city, and fire came down from heaven and devoured them" (Revelation 20:9, NASB).

The camp of the saints—the Holy City, our heavenly home—is now on earth. How will it get here after the millennium? God's plan is totally amazing. "Now I saw a new heaven and a new earth, for the first heaven and the first earth had passed away. Also there was no more sea. Then I, John, saw the holy city, New Jerusalem, coming down out of heaven from God, prepared as a bride adorned for her husband" (Revelation 21:1, 2).

This is better than *Star Trek!* The New Jerusalem is like a giant space city, descending from heaven with the saints inside. It settles on Mount of Olives, the site of present Jerusalem (Zechariah 14:4). Now everyone who has ever lived will be alive on earth at the same time—inside or outside the New Jerusalem.

Imagine the sight as Satan compares his vast army with the much smaller group within the city. He has military leaders from all history behind him. I think I can see Hitler, along with famous generals who never lost a battle. Satan rallies his forces for a final furious attack on God's throne in the Holy City. The huge army of rebels moves forward.

What happens next? Hellfire. "Fire comes down from heaven and devours" the wicked. The earth becomes a boiling lake of fire as God cleanses it from sin.

Did you notice the intriguing parallel between the flood destroying the world in Noah's day and the fire of earth's final destruction? Just as Noah's ark rode upon the waters of the Flood, so the Holy City with the saints inside will withstand the lake of fire. Hellfire will be hot, so hot that sin and sinners will not survive. But after those flames have done their cleansing work, they will go out. Remember how the water receded in Noah's day and the ark settled back down on the earth? The lake of fire will subside like that, and the Holy City will stand upon a purified planet.

Keep in mind that back in Noah's day when the people drowned, they were gone. God didn't keep them endlessly thrashing about in the water. And the citizens of ancient Sodom and Gomorrah aren't still burning, over there beneath the Dead Sea. But doesn't the Bible say that Sodom and Gomorrah were destroyed by "eternal fire"? Yes. In Jude 7 we find that those cities were "exhibited as an example, in undergoing the punishment of eternal fire" (NASB).

Eternal Punish*ment*, Not Punish*ing*

Eternal fire is eternal in its effect. The punish*ment* is everlasting—but not the punish*ing,* with the eternal fire "turning the cities of Sodom and Gomorrah into ashes, . . . making them an example to those who afterward would live ungodly" (2 Peter 2:6).

Remember, the wages of sin is death—not eternal life in hell (Romans 6:23). Death means the absence of life, the absence of existence. Only those who have the Son have life; those who haven't accepted Jesus don't have life to spend anywhere, either in heaven or hell.

So the doctrine of eternal hell isn't based upon Scripture. It's yet another false teaching from the Middle Ages that has stayed within the church. In addition to being unbiblical, eternal torment doesn't make sense. Think about it. If God would punish in the flames someone who simply neglected salvation as long as He punishes Hitler or Idi Amin, how could He be a God of justice? Suppose our legal system were to sentence every offender with the same jail term, speeders and murderers alike. None of us would consider that fair—and yet it's exactly what many people imagine God will do.

Here's another point to consider. On the cross Jesus paid the wages of the whole world's sin by His death. Did Jesus suffer eternal torment? Of course not—at least not as time goes. Then to say sinners must be eternally punished suggests that our Savior failed to pay the full price of their sin.

Then what does the Bible mean about the smoke of their torment ascending up forever? We must let the Bible interpret its own terms. Did you know that Scripture uses the word "forever" more than 50 times for things already ended? For instance, in 1 Samuel 1:22 we read that the prophet Samuel's mother promised him as a gift to the Lord "forever." Yet verse 28 explains, "as long as he lives he shall be lent to the Lord."

So there we have it. As long as the wicked live, as long as consciousness lasts, they will burn. For some it may be just a few moments. Others will suffer longer. Yet even Satan himself will be finished off at last.

All who reject their Savior's death must finally themselves perish. For the good of the universe, for the good of everyone concerned, every trace of sin will be erased.

New Earth Paradise

At last Christ's long-awaited promise can be fulfilled that "the meek" will "inherit the earth" (Matthew 5:5). Not this old polluted planet, but an earth made new. Before that can happen, "'the proud, yes, all who do wickedly, will be stubble. And the day which is coming shall burn them up,' says the Lord of hosts, 'that will leave them neither root nor branch. . . . You shall trample the wicked, for they shall be ashes under the soles of your feet on the day that I do this,' says the Lord of hosts" (Malachi 4:1-3).

Then God brings beauty out of ashes, re-creating the breathtaking magnificence of long-lost Eden. Finally the rebellion is over, never to trouble a peaceful universe again. Sin exists no longer, and gone with it are death and disappointment and pain. Then God will present this born-again planet to His people as our eternal paradise home. "And I heard a loud voice from heaven saying, 'Behold, the tabernacle of God is with men, and He will dwell with them, and they shall be His people. God Himself will be with them and be their God. And God will wipe away every tear from their eyes; there shall be no more death, nor sorrow, nor crying. There shall be no more pain, for the former things have passed away.' Then He who sat on the throne said, 'Behold, I make all things new'" (Revelation 21:3-5).

So God will move the capital city of the universe from heaven down to our little planet. Why? Because He so loved the world that He *gave* us His only Son. For all eternity the Son of Man will remain one of us, our brother in humanity as well as our Lord! And Jerusalem on this earth, where Jesus suffered and died for our salvation, will be God's capital city from which He governs the universe. God Himself will dwell with us forever.

The King Is Coming!

The Bible truth about God's plan for His people and this planet is terrific news. We don't need to embellish it with fictional speculation about prophecy. And remember, there is no second chance for those left behind when Jesus comes. Now is the time to book your travel arrangements to heaven.

If you have already accepted Jesus, are you committed to follow Him obediently wherever He leads you in His Word?

Yes, Christ is coming! If this does not fit into your plans, then by all means change your plans. God will help you.

Chapter 6

DESECRATION
OF THE TEMPLE

Could Nicolae Carpathia be the Messiah?
The prospect seems exciting . . . intriguing . . .
compelling. Full of grace and power, Carpathia is unlike
any man on earth. Everybody seems enamored of his
compassion and vision for global unity. Plus, he's got
the leadership to pull everyone together and restore sta-
bility in the aftermath of the mass disappearances. Now
longtime enemies are becoming partners for peace.

Also amazing—miraculous, actually—is Nicolae
Carpathia's appearance on the world scene. Just a
month earlier he had been an obscure legislator in
Romania. Then he rose to the presidency of that nation. Suddenly he is the dynamic secretary-general of
the United Nations and immediately proceeds to win
the allegiance of world leaders, even the president of
the United States. Propelled to ever greater heights by
his character and charisma, apparently without political maneuvering, Nicolae becomes the most popular
person on the planet. He seems humble yet talented,
gentle yet forceful, unselfish yet ambitious—not for
himself but for the benefit of the new Global
Community, of course.

DESECRATION OF THE TEMPLE

At sidewalk cafés, supermarkets, and TV talk shows, the consensus is obvious: What more could you expect from a messiah than what we have in Nicolae Carpathia?

Pastor Bruce Barnes and fellow members of the Trib Force dissent from popular opinion. Being staunch believers, they realize that the title of messiah belongs exclusively to Jesus Christ. They see Carpathia as a lion waiting to pounce on unsuspecting prey. But few others suspect that he is a scheming, satanic dictator anticipating his moment to strike. And so the nations of the world, falling over themselves to cooperate with Nicolae, are putting the finishing touches on his plans for global disarmament and one-world currency. Leaders of the various world religions are lining up behind his proposal of one universal religion to be headed by Peter Matthews, Rome's newly elected supreme pope, upon whom Nicolae bestows the old Roman title "Pontifex Maximus." Even skeptical Israelis are fooled into seeking Carpathia as a friend with their best good in mind.

Now all eyes are on Israel for the signing of a historic treaty with Nicolae Carpathia that guarantees not only its survival and prosperity, but also the fulfillment of every observant Jew's fond prayer: the rebuilding of the Temple in Jerusalem.

But what about Islam's Dome of the Rock, which occupies the Temple Mount, where the Jews must erect their own temple?

We'll consider later Nicolae's creative solution to that dilemma, but first let's take a break for some perspective.

Horrific Desecration

The scenario you just read belongs to the *Left*

Behind version of final events. It's part of a broader out-line: Soon after the rapture Nicolae the antichrist's covenant with the Jews enables the resumption of an-cient temple services in Jerusalem—complete with ani-mal sacrifices for sin. Three and a half years later Carpathia suddenly breaks his covenant with Israel. He desecrates the temple by sacrificing a pig on the altar, proclaiming himself the one and only true god. Jewish worshipers are horrified. Their eyes are opened to Carpathia's deceptions, and they revolt against him. He in turn wages war against Israel. Millions of unbelieving Jews come to Christ and accept Him as their Messiah. They stand firm throughout the Great Tribulation, which culminates in the Battle of Armageddon and the final glorious appearance of Jesus Christ. Then follows the millennial reign of Christ and the saints.

Central to this concept of final events is the re-building of the Jewish temple. Other than the rapture itself at the beginning of the seven years and Christ's final glorious appearing at the end, it is perhaps the most anticipated event of prophecy for millions of sincere Christians, including the authors of the *Left Behind* series. The importance attributed to the rebuilt temple deserves our attention in this chapter.

We begin with some historical background about Jerusalem's Temple Mount.

Dealing With the Dome

The anticipated new Jewish worship center would be built on Jerusalem's Temple Mount. For two millennia, this morsel of real estate has seen the fiercest turf wars in the history of the world. Jews, Muslims, and Christians consider it sacred.

Jewish tradition identifies it as Mount Moriah, where Abraham was willing to literally sacrifice Isaac at God's command. They also regard its location as supremely sacred because their ancestors worshiped at this same spot in the Temple that King Solomon built. Then, 600 years before Christ was born in nearby Bethlehem, the Babylonian army destroyed Jerusalem's first Temple. But, as we saw earlier, another Temple replaced it, which later was extravagantly enlarged by Herod the Great.

Christians cherish the site because Jesus frequented the Temple precincts when He was present in Jerusalem. The biblical book of Acts gives evidence that the first Christians, especially those who lived in Jerusalem, honored the Temple and even worshiped there (see Acts 2:46; 3:1).

In chapter 2 we discussed the destruction of the Temple by the Roman army in the year A.D. 70. With that Temple destroyed and Jerusalem in ruins, Jewish people were scattered across the Roman [...] a tragic loss to God's historic and ancien[...]

Subsequently, on three separate [...] Jews entertained plans to rebuild [...] During the revolt led by Bar Kokhba (A[...] pious Jews began putting together pl[...] their ancient place of worship, even [...] bearing a likeness of the restored Temp[...] and 363, under the impetus given by E[...] "The Apostate," Jews returned to Je[...] they had hopes of rebuilding the Tem[...] A.D. 614, during the Byzantine Empi[...] returned the control of Jerusalem to t[...] more plans were underfoot to re[...] Temple, but there was little success, an[...] Jerusalem was returned to Christian do[...]

When Muslims eventually conqu[...] with its Temple Mount, they were th[...]

vere the spot because their tradition tells them that one night Muhammad rode a winged steed from Mecca to this very spot, from which he ascended to heaven. Between A.D. 687 and 691 Caliph Abd al-Malik ibn Marwān constructed the Dome of the Rock, also known as the Mosque of Omar, a misnomer because Omar is not the one who constructed this shrine. Adjacent to the Dome of the Rock is the Al-Aqsā Mosque, built in A.D. 710 by Caliph al-Walid.

For many centuries the fate of Jerusalem swung back and forth like a pendulum. Various popes commissioned Crusades to win back Jerusalem. Christian armies stormed through the Mediterranean area, gaining and then losing possession of the city. As the twentieth century dawned, Islamic Palestinians controlled the Holy Land, with a few Jewish settlers trickling in. More Jews immigrated after World War I. Following World War II, refugees from the European Holocaust returned to their ancient homeland, where they established a nation in 1948. During the dramatic Six Day War of 1967, the Israelis recaptured Jerusalem.

Among first-century Christians, the destruction of the Temple was not viewed as a terrible tragedy, as it was among first-century Jews, because their religious perspective did not require worship and sacrifice at the Temple.

"The early church at the end of the first century and later placed no emphasis on the notion that the Temple might one day be restored" (*The Anchor Bible Dictionary*, vol. 6, p. 367). Even later, "In the Byzantine period, when Jerusalem was largely a Christian city, no steps were taken, despite the flurry of construction work that characterized the fourth to sixth centuries, to clear the ruins on the Temple Mount let alone to restore it" (*ibid.*).

DESECRATION OF THE TEMPLE

The Christians had "strong theological reasons for the neglect of the temple building. . . . The ongoing cycle of sacrificial offerings and especially the annual sin offering were epitomized and fulfilled, once and for all, by the sacrifice of Jesus' life. . . . [This] ruled out forever the need for further sacrifices at either an earthly or heavenly temple (see Heb. 8:10)" *(ibid.)*.

And although the first-century Jews regarded the destruction of their Temple as a great and tragic loss, even for many of them the disappointment that resulted from its destruction was mollified somewhat because they felt that because the Temple was not merely "mundane, it could never be completely destroyed. It continued to exist in Judaism in present reality through Torah" *(ibid.)*.

Nevertheless, many Jews kept alive the hope that someday the Temple would be reconstructed—as it had been so many centuries earlier. We have already taken notice of their three abortive attempts to rebuild the Temple as late as the seventh century. But now in a new millennium, many Jews believe that God has given Jerusalem back to them in preparation for rebuilding the Temple. Despite both Christian and Jewish theological reasons that the loss of the Temple is not a strategic problem for their ongoing worship of the true God, today many Jews join millions of Christians in believing that a rebuilt temple would fulfill the prophetic blueprint.

There's just one obstacle—a huge one. The Temple Mount remains occupied by Muslims. In fact, the Dome of the Rock is one of Islam's holiest shrines. Muslims everywhere would die in a heartbeat to prevent Jews from rebuilding a temple there, which would result in the desecration and destruction of two of their revered sites—the Dome of the Rock and the Al-Aqsā Mosque. Anyone who does not reckon with Islamic zeal on this matter is simply naive.

So what will happen? The *Left Behind* authors suggest that the antichrist will persuade Muslims to allow their two sacred edifices to be relocated to New Babylon, headquarters of the Global Community. Carpathia's successful resolution of this age-old dilemma convinces many Jews, even the Orthodox, that he is indeed Messiah. That is, until he breaks his covenant with Israel after just three and a half short years.

However unlikely the possibility that Muslims would let their Dome of the Rock be relocated from Jerusalem's Temple Mount, we can acknowledge the authors' creativity in conceiving such a solution. But such a move would not really solve the temple problem from a biblical perspective, since Babylon in Bible prophecy represents a corrupted, compromised Christianity, not a geographical location in modern Iraq.

We'll address this in a future chapter. For now, let's focus on Jerusalem and its Temple.

Preparing for a New Temple

The *Left Behind* authors have written another book in which they assert: "Anyone interested in end-time events has his eyes on the temple project" (Tim LaHaye and Jerry B. Jenkins, *Are We Living in the End Times?*, p. 123).

They cite various projects said to be under way in preparing for the rebuilt Jerusalem Temple. One of their examples is the Temple Mount Faithful, a Jewish organization whose spokesman during a recent tour of America gave interviews to many Christian broadcasters, including Pat Robertson for his *700 Club* (*ibid.*, p. 124).

Another such group is the Temple Institute, which has constructed almost all the 102 utensils needed for Temple worship according to biblical and rabbinic standards, including garments for priests, musical instruments, vessels for carrying blood, a brazen laver, and so on. Some of these items are on display at their tourist center in the Old City of Jerusalem.

What about priests to administer the new Temple? The *Left Behind* authors report that the organization Ateret Cohanim has established a yeshiva, or religious school, for training Temple priests. Indeed, according to an Associated Press report, a Jerusalem-based religious group called the Movement for Establishing the Temple has been recruiting ultra-Orthodox parents to dedicate their boys to the Jewish priestly class known as *Cohenim*. (*Kohen* is the Hebrew word for priest.)

Assuming the accuracy of these reports, preparations are well under way for the temple itself, its utensils, and even priests in training. What about sacrificial animals? Recently there was a flurry of excitement over the discovery of a red heifer allegedly without blemishes, named Melody, originally believed to be the first of its kind born in the Holy Land in two millennia. But later, white hairs were spotted on the young cow's tail, and she was deemed impure. (Rabbinic tradition insisted that a single white hair on a red heifer kept it from being used as a sacrifice.)

Melody's disqualification brought a sigh of relief to many in Israel. "'That cow represents the risk of a massive religious war,' said Avraham Poraz, a member of the parliament from the leftist Meretz Party. 'If the fanatics get ahold of it and try to take over the Temple Mount, God knows what will happen.'"

Indeed, only God knows what the zealots will

risk in matters related to rebuilding the Temple. They are confident that soon they will have their red heifer. Millions of Christians are praying that they do.

Does Bible prophecy endorse this excitement about red heifers and a renewed priesthood in a re-built Jewish temple? Let's consider several problems with this scenario.

Jesus, the Only Sacrifice

What really disqualified Melody the cow from serving as a valid sacrifice for sin was not a white hair or two in her tail. On the cross 2,000 years ago Jesus Christ became the full and final sacrifice for sin: "Behold! The Lamb of God who takes away the sin of the world!" (John 1:29).

"But Christ came as High Priest of the good things to come, with the greater and more perfect tabernacle not made with hands, that is, not of this creation. Not with the blood of goats and calves, but with His own blood He entered the Most Holy Place once for all, having obtained eternal redemption. For if the blood of bulls and goats and the ashes of a heifer . . . sanctifies for the purifying of the flesh, how much more shall the blood of Christ, who through the eter-nal Spirit offered Himself without spot to God, cleanse your conscience from dead works to serve the living God?" (Hebrews 9:11-14).

So all this enthusiasm about a red cow amounts to nothing but "dead works." Sacrificing animals in a new temple does not square well with the testimony found in the New Testament and amounts to false re-ligion. Blasphemy, in fact.

The *Left Behind* authors recognize this fact. Being solid evangelicals, they acknowledge that the concept of a rebuilt temple in Jerusalem is an abomination in light of the one and only sacrifice of Jesus Christ (Tim LaHaye and Jerry B. Jenkins, *Apollyon,* p. 14).

Tim LaHaye furthermore realizes that the Jews' interest in such a temple evidences continued rejection of Christ (*Revelation Unveiled,* p. 185). But then the *Left Behind* authors apparently contradict their own Christian faith. They describe this counterfeit temple as having a "sacred altar" (Tim LaHaye and Jerry B. Jenkins, *The Mark*), which the antichrist defiles by sacrificing a pig on it. In reality, any sacrifice other than Christ's—even that of a kosher cow—would compete with Calvary and thus defile the temple.

Yet Tim LaHaye, perhaps unintentionally, includes Jewish animal sacrifices in the same category as the sacrifice of Christ when he says: "Israel, Christians, and Tribulation saints share in common this essential: They enter into a covenant with God by sacrifice, the covenant of a blood sacrifice—Israel temporarily by animal sacrifices; Christians and the Tribulation saints through the Lord Jesus Christ, who sacrificed Himself 'once for all'" (*Unveiled,* p. 195).

Since Christ's sacrifice is uniquely valid, animal sacrifice is not "essential" but totally illegitimate. *Even temporarily,* such a sacrifice would be blasphemous, long before the antichrist totes his pig into the Temple.

Totally apart from any of its sacrifices, the involvement of the antichrist in building a temple defiles the place, right from the start. This raises the question How can the antichrist and his pig desecrate this rebuilt temple later on, *since it is already unholy—and always has been?*

Another difficulty with *Left Behind* theology is its identification of the antichrist's temple as "the Temple of God" (quoting 2 Thessalonians 2:1-13). And yet Tim LaHaye also accurately points out that God's temple on earth is not a building, since our body is the temple of the Holy Spirit (*ibid.,* p. 185). Yes, we as the body of Christ are the "temple of God" on earth. Surely this proves that the antichrist will operate from within the Christian Church, like Judas, and not from within some counterfeit temple in Jerusalem. You recall we discussed this in chapter 3.

The *Left Behind* authors say that the antichrist will attack his own temple and end its animal sacrifices, which they describe as the "abomination of desolation" (Daniel 9:27). Actually, if the antichrist puts to a stop the blasphemous sacrificing of animals, it would be a blessing of desolation, *not an abomination* of desolation. (If you are unclear about what the abomination of desolation really is, you might want to reread chapter 2 of this book.)

For all these reasons and more, the *Left Behind* prophetic scenario suffers incompatibility with the gospel faith of its own authors. Students of Bible prophecy have no reason to focus on a temple in Jerusalem. When Jesus completed His sacrifice on the cross, according to the witness of the New Testament, this ended forever the significance of the earthly, typical Temple and its sacrifices. When God tore apart the sacred curtain of the Jewish Temple upon Jesus' death, this should have provided a clear omen that these symbolic services had been fulfilled by Jesus' death and thus had lost their figurative meaning. Any discussion today about a Jerusalem temple is wasted energy. In fact, it is a diversion of the devil.

Let's discover the truth about what the Bible says about Christ's work in heaven for us.

Jesus, the Only High Priest

With 2,000 years having passed since Christ's sacrifice for our sin, how do we connect with its benefits today? The Bible says, "We have an *Advocate* with the Father, Jesus Christ the righteous" (1 John 2:1). "For there is one God and one *Mediator* between God and men, the Man Christ Jesus" (1 Timothy 2:5). "It is Christ who died, and furthermore is also risen, who is even at the right hand of God, who also makes *intercession* for us" (Romans 8:34).

So Jesus is our advocate, mediator, and intercessor. These different words are synonyms describing His ministry as our high priest at heaven's throne of mercy, providing us grace and help in time of need. When we are overwhelmed by guilt, fear, weakness, or confusion, we can come with confidence to God through Jesus, our intercessor. No enemy has the right to blame us or shame us. It's Christ's ministry to defend us against all attacks and accusations. Anyone claiming to be another high priest in some rebuilt temple would be a competitor, a counterfeit of Christ. And didn't Jesus Himself warn against such impostors in the last days? (See Matthew 24:24.)

According to the New Testament, "Christ has not entered the holy places made with hands, . . . but into heaven itself, now to appear in the presence of God for us" (Hebrews 9:24). This truth about Christ's work for us in heaven's sanctuary has been tragically neglected, even though it has great importance. "This is the main point of the things we are saying: We have such a High Priest, who is seated at the right hand of the throne of the Majesty in the heavens, a Minister of the sanctuary and of the true tabernacle which the Lord erected, and not man" (Hebrews 8:1, 2). So any temple on earth built by human hands would then be an unauthorized imitation, unauthorized, that is, by God.

DESECRATION, DANGER, DELIVERANCE

Looking Up to Jesus

Jerusalem has the richest history and heritage of any city in the world. When London, Paris, and Washington, D.C., were still forests and meadows, Jerusalem was the center of God's salvation activity. But remember, this changed after Jesus died on the cross, rose from the dead, and ascended to heaven's New Jerusalem (Revelation 21:2). And so the New Testament calls away from "the present city of Jerusalem, because she is in slavery with her children. But the Jerusalem that is above is free, and she is our mother" (Galatians 4:25, 26, NIV). "You have come to . . . the heavenly Jerusalem, . . . to Jesus the Mediator of the new covenant" (Hebrews 12:22-24).

Unfortunately, many Christians are completely uninformed about Jesus' high priestly work at God's throne, the antitypical temple. Nothing can be clearer than this: True prophecy points to Jesus in the heavenly holy places of the New Jerusalem, whereas false prophecy anticipates events in a counterfeit temple built by human hands in old Jerusalem.

Don't put your hope in an earthly city, temple, or nation. Focus on Jesus in heaven and anchor your faith up there. Only then will you be safe, never to be left behind.

Chapter 7

THE OTHER COVENANT

Nicolae is worried.

Jerusalem is heavy on his heart. All the cities of the world have fallen under his spell except the Jewish holy city. And now Tribulation saints from around the world are flocking into Israel for the Conference of Witnesses. Leading the way are the 144,000 Jewish missionaries on fire for God. Carpathia is clearly threatened by their testimony, and plots to undermine it.

Such is the *Left Behind* scenario midway between the rapture and Christ's final glorious appearing.

Actually, Jerusalem has historically been a hotbed of religious zeal for the children of Abraham. These days radical Muslims bomb Jewish shopping centers and school buses in their fervor for Allah. They consider themselves the true children of Abraham ("Ibrahim," they call him) because Ishmael their forefather was his firstborn son. Is their claim valid?

No. Ishmael was conceived outside the covenant of faith that God had established with Abraham. This immediately disqualifies Islam from the covenant. The Bible is clear: "Know that *only those who are of faith are* sons of Abraham" (Galatians 3:7). So the only hope for Muslims to become true children of Abraham is to reflect his faith in the Messiah of the covenant.

How about the Jews? They too descended from Abraham, but through Isaac, the faith-child through whom God's covenant was to be fulfilled. Does having Isaac as one's ancestor mean that Jews can automatically claim Abraham as their spiritual father?

Since we said no about the Muslims, it is tempting to say yes about the Jews. But let's not rush to any conclusions. The same question came up back in Jesus' day. Jewish religious leaders felt no need of Jesus Christ because they claimed a secure status as the seed of Abraham (through Isaac), God's chosen people. Jesus disagreed: "If you were Abraham's children, you would do the works of Abraham" (John 8:39). Evidently having a genetic bond with Abraham is not enough to qualify as his children, whether one has descended from Ishmael or Isaac. The true descendants qualify only if they share the active faith of Abraham in the Messiah of the covenant.

Faith in the Messiah of the covenant is not optional. Enlightened Bible scholars know that *the Old Testament is not primarily Israel-centered, but Messiah-centered*. Everything depends upon accepting Christ. "For all the promises of God in Him are Yes, and in Him Amen, to the glory of God" (2 Corinthians 1:20). Without a relationship with Jesus Christ, nobody has access to God's covenant promises; nobody can claim to be the chosen of God.

Chosen in Christ

This matter of a chosen people has raised questions such as, Does God play favorites? No. Scripture says "that God shows no partiality" (Acts 10:34). He doesn't value one ethnic group above another. So in what sense were the Jews His chosen people?

Let's get some background on this. Long ago God chose Abraham for a specific purpose. "In you all the families of the earth shall be blessed" (Genesis 12:3). So the Lord wanted to use Abraham and his descendants to be channels of blessing to the whole world— Exhibit A of blessings shared through a faith community. He wasn't playing favorites, automatically blessing one group while prejudiced against others. Through one group He intended to bless everyone.

The church, however, has not related well to the Jews. Protestants and Catholics alike have often despised and defamed them. Centuries of anti-Semitism climaxed in the Nazi Holocaust, with mainline German churches complicit with Hitler and often totally supportive. Anti-Semitism continues today, although many Christians have shifted to the opposite extreme by exalting the Jews as if they were heaven's automatic favorites.

Let's remember that God's purpose for choosing Israel was not to create an elite nation but to serve as His channel of blessing to the whole world. Instead, the Jews historically have hoarded the blessings of Abraham's covenant for themselves. Back when Christ walked this earth, Jews forbade Gentiles on penalty of death from even worshiping side by side with them. Back in 1871 archaeologists uncovered evidence of this death decree. Digging among the ruins of the Temple site in Jerusalem, they found the very stone marked with the following warning in both Hebrew and Greek: "No man of another race is to proceed within the partition and enclosing wall about the sanctuary. And one arrested there will have himself to blame for the penalty of death which will be imposed as a consequence."

Jesus did not view this threat as appropriate. He said, "Is it not written, 'My house shall be called a house of prayer for all nations'?" (Mark 11:17). He was actually quoting the Bible—the Hebrew Scriptures, which quote God as stating: "My house shall be called a house of prayer for all nations" (Isaiah 56:7).

How tragic! At best, Jews treated the Gentiles with aloofness; at worst, they despised them. And the Gentiles responded in the same spirit, regarding the Jews as enemies of the human race. But Jesus broke through that wall. Two thousand years ago He came down from heaven to abolish the barrier dividing Jew from Gentile. Refusing to pander to national prejudice, He visited Gentile villages, associating with people whom the Pharisees considered to be unclean. His life was a constant attempt to level differences and to unify people at enmity with one another.

Through His death He ultimately achieved this: "But now in Christ Jesus you who once were far off have been brought near by the blood of Christ. For He Himself is our peace, who has made both one, and has broken down the middle wall of separation, . . . so as to create in Himself one new man from the two" (Ephesians 2:13-15).

Jesus united Jew and Gentile by creating in Himself a new humanity. This is actually a new human people—Christ's body, the church. Most Christians are completely unaware of this. Yet *Jesus Himself is now the new Israel*. He personally is the Seed of Abraham (Galatians 3:16), and we all are God's elect in Jesus, His chosen ones through the gospel. "There is neither Jew nor Greek, there is neither slave nor free, there is neither male nor female; for you are all one in Christ Jesus" (verse 28).

The Bible is plain: In Christ there is no longer any

distinction between Jew and Gentile. Whoever would make such a distinction is unwittingly denying the gospel. The same is true for anyone who clings to any type of prejudice or chauvinism, whether related to race, gender, socioeconomic status, political power, or any other distinction. "For in Christ Jesus you are all children of God through faith" (verse 26, NRSV). He has commissioned His church to gather Jews and Gentiles together into a fellowship of love and life in the salvation covenant.

Jewish Response to the Gospel

How has the Jewish nation responded to all this? What have they done with God's gift of the Messiah?

Jimmy Carter, former United States president, recounts a trip to Israel in his book *The Blood of Abraham*. He tells of visiting several kibbutzim, or Jewish settlements, near the Sea of Galilee. One Sabbath he dropped in on the local synagogue in a community of several hundred and was shocked to find only two other worshipers present.

Later when the Carters visited Prime Minister Golda Meir, the conversation drifted to religion. Carter commented about the general lack of spiritual interest among the Israelis. The prime minister agreed but said she wasn't concerned because of the Orthodox Jews in the nation. She added with a laugh, "If you attend a session of the Knesset [the Israeli parliament], you will see them in action and will know they have not lost their faith" (pp. 8, 9).

Granted that Orthodox Jews today have not lost their zeal. But could we call it faith? Perhaps it is more accurate to ask, Faith in what? In their Messiah, Jesus Christ?

Tragically, the situation today is the same as it was

2,000 years ago. "His own did not receive Him" (John 1:11). Yet even after Jewish leaders played an instrumental role in the death of their Messiah, God's mercy lingered. Instead of immediately sending His disciples around the Roman Empire with the gospel, the resurrected Christ sent them first to "the lost sheep of the house of Israel," beginning with Jerusalem. Remember, the Jewish nation still had left to them three and a half years of national probation—the last half of the seventieth week in Daniel 9. But time was short. Those 490 years of opportunity to accept the covenant would expire in A.D. 34.

What did Israel do with its final years of opportunity? Thousands of individual Jews accepted Jesus, according to the testimony recorded in the biblical book of Acts, but nationally the covenant God had initiated had been rejected. After stoning God's messenger, Stephen (Acts 7), they launched a great persecution against fellow Jews who believed in Jesus. At this point the apostles declared: "It was necessary that the word of God should be spoken to you first; but since you reject it, and judge yourselves unworthy of everlasting life, behold, we turn to the Gentiles" (Acts 13:46).

Jesus had warned Jewish leaders this would happen: "The kingdom of God will be *taken from you* and given to a nation bearing the fruits of it" (Matthew 21:43). So now the covenant promises are removed from the nation of Israel *as a whole* and given to all believers in Jesus, both Jews and Gentiles. "If you are Christ's, then you are Abraham's seed, and heirs according to the promise" (Galatians 3:29).

Many Jews today are indeed children of Abraham, not because of their genealogies but through their faith in Jesus as Messiah. Multitudes more will, according to Scripture, accept Him. Abraham's covenant now belongs not to one particular nation but to anyone who believes in Jesus.

Can non-Jews really become children of Abraham? Corporately in Christ, yes. "You are a chosen generation, a royal priesthood, a holy nation, His own special people . . . who once were not a people but are now the people of God" (1 Peter 2:9, 10).

Has God rejected the Jews? No (Romans 11:1, 2). The nation as a whole rejected Him. In Christ's day "the Pharisees and experts in the law rejected God's purpose for themselves" (Luke 7:30, NIV). After Pentecost they squandered their last years of national probation. In two millennia since then, little has changed in the general Jewish attitude toward Jesus. But God has not abandoned His idea of a covenant people, which Paul likens to an olive tree. Because of unbelief, the Jewish branches in Paul's day had been pruned from the tree, and Gentiles who believed had been grafted in (Romans 11:20, 24). Yet even now *as individuals* both Jews and Gentiles can be grafted into the tree representing God's covenant people—the church, the body of Christ (verses 23, 24).

To understand this, remember that any covenant is a partnership, an agreement between two parties with conditions for both to fulfill. Like the covenant of marriage, for example. Bride and groom stand at the altar exchanging vows, making a covenant together. Both agree to live by its terms—as long as life lasts—or the covenant is forfeited.

Just so with the covenant between the Lord and the Jewish nation. More is involved than merely a faithful God keeping His promise. His people also must be faithful, abiding by the terms of the covenant. *All of God's covenant promises are conditional upon human cooperation.* (See Jeremiah 18:7-10; Deuteronomy 28.)

DESECRATION, DANGER, DELIVERANCE

Six centuries before Christ, God's messenger Jeremiah predicted that unrepentant Jerusalem would fall prey to Babylon. But Hananiah, a popular religious teacher, opposed Heaven's warning of doom. This false prophet assured the rebellious nation that they had nothing to worry about. After all, God had unconditionally promised through Isaiah that He would bless Jerusalem, so that promise must stand no matter what—whether or not the nation repented.

Jeremiah faithfully rebuked the false prophets. "They continually say to those who despise Me, 'The Lord has said, "You shall have peace"'; and to everyone who walks according to the imagination of his own heart, 'No evil shall come upon you'" (Jeremiah 23:17).

Evidently, false prophets in the Old Testament insisted that God would fulfill His covenant regardless of the way His people behaved. Do we hear echoes of the same teaching today among certain Christian groups?

What made the difference between true and false prophecy in Israel's history? True prophets stressed that the nation must repent to receive the covenant blessings. False prophets said God had guaranteed to bless Jerusalem no matter what. It wasn't just a matter of those who talked about God and those who did not. It actually boiled down to the issue of what they said about God's covenant people. Being part of God's covenant people meant being part of a believing and faithful community.

History repeated itself. Just before the destruction of Jerusalem in A.D. 70, false prophets again arose. They promised the unbelieving, disloyal nation deliverance from enemy attacks. Josephus, the Jewish historian living at the time, reported that such false messengers encouraged presumptuous patriotism—until that final fatal moment when Roman soldiers stormed Jerusalem. The unrepentant citizens perished with their false prophets.

Jesus, years in advance, had warned His followers to flee from the doomed city of Jerusalem, which they did. We would do well to take our Lord's advice today—flee from false prophecies about Jerusalem.

False faith (sometimes called presumption) in Jerusalem brought ruin in Old Testament times and then again in New Testament times. Will it happen again today?

The Two Covenants

Now we can clear up some further confusion about God's covenant. Many believe that in Old Testament times God planned back then to save Israel by their works, but then in New Testament times and since He has switched things around, saving us now by grace and through faith.

But isn't there an old covenant that is different from the new covenant? Good question. Let's find out what the Bible teaches.

The first mention of a covenant in the Bible is in Genesis, when the world became so wicked that God had to destroy it with a flood. "But Noah found grace in the eyes of the Lord" (Genesis 6:8). Based on that grace, the Lord spared Noah's life and established with him a treaty of spiritual partnership known as the "everlasting covenant" (Genesis 9:16).

Later God approached Abraham with this same everlasting covenant (Genesis 17:7). One night He called Abraham outside his tent and urged him to look upward toward the desert sky. "See the stars?" God asked. "So shall your descendants be." Abraham "believed in the Lord, and He accounted it to him for righteousness" (Genesis 15:5, 6). So Abraham's covenant was based on belief, not works. The gospel of grace runs clear through the Old Testament like a refreshing mountain stream.

Picture the scene of Abraham with his son Isaac climbing Mount Moriah, that mountain of sacrifice. The aged father trembled at the thought of losing his only son. Then he remembered the gospel: "My son, God will provide for Himself the lamb for a burnt of-fering" (Genesis 22:8).

God Himself provides the sacrifice for sin. That's our hope today. And their hope too, those who lived way back during those times depicted in Genesis and Exodus.

Unfortunately, Abraham's descendants forgot the gospel while suffering as slaves in Egypt. But in their distress they cried out to Heaven. "God heard their groaning, and God remembered His covenant with Abraham" (Exodus 2:24). Through one of the most dramatic events of history—opening up the Red Sea—God delivered them from bondage.

After bringing His people safely across, God led them in the desert to Mount Sinai. In that majestic setting He intended to renew with them the same ev-erlasting covenant of grace already established with Noah and Abraham. He introduced the covenant by reminding His people of what He had just graciously done to save them: "You have seen what *I did* to the Egyptians, and how *I* . . . brought you to Myself. Now therefore, if you will indeed obey My voice and keep My covenant, then you shall be a special treasure to Me" (Exodus 19:4, 5).

God wanted the Israelites to accept *His* work for their salvation. But somehow they failed to connect with His grace and power, despite good intentions.

The results were tragic. A few days after they had promised, "All that the Lord says we will do" (verse 8), the very same people were dancing around in a wild orgy, worshiping a golden calf. Picture the scene! All their promises and resolutions lay shattered in the desert sand.

Humbled and chastened, the Israelites were finally ready to hear the gospel. God explained the meaning of sacrificial lambs, just as He had done with Adam and Eve at the gates of the Garden of Eden. Every bleeding lamb on the altar was to remind them to trust for salvation in the blood of their Savior to come.

Centuries later, when Jesus came to this earth, He fulfilled a new covenant. A covenant based upon "better promises" than the old covenant established at Sinai (Hebrews 8:6). Better promises because God made them, not frail humanity.

Here's something interesting: Christ's sacrifice was the "blood of the everlasting covenant" (Hebrews 13:20). Actually, it's the same covenant of grace established long ago with Noah and Abraham. It's called the new covenant here because God reconfirmed it at the cross—whereas the old covenant had been ratified back at Sinai. (See Exodus 24:8.)

Notice the promise of this new or everlasting covenant: "'This is the covenant that I will make with them after those days, says the Lord: I will put My laws into their hearts, and in their minds I will write them,' then He adds, 'Their sins and their lawless deeds I will remember no more'" (Hebrews 10:16, 17).

Some suggest that under the new covenant God's law is abolished. But here we read just the opposite: What had been engraved on tables of stone under the old covenant is now written in our minds and hearts under the new covenant. Yet notice that it ends with forgiveness. Even though faithful hearts honor all God's commandments, we continually need mercy to cover our shortcomings.

Certain things changed through Christ's provision of the new covenant. Christian baptism replaced the act of circumcision, and the Lord's Supper took the place of the Passover feast. (You may recall that the first Lord's Supper took place during Passover time.)

Other things never changed, as we'll see in our next chapter. But first let's wrap up our study on God's chosen people.

Satan's Final Deception

These days we see lots of excitement about the country of Israel. None could deny that remarkable things have happened there since 1948. But how can these events qualify as a fulfillment of God's covenant to Abraham when Israel as a nation still rejects Jesus? Sharing the gospel is next to impossible there, especially in Jerusalem. Even full-blooded Jews who trust in Jesus as Messiah have not been welcome in Israel to the same immigration benefits as unbelievers.

Well, if the fulfillment of God's covenant to Abraham is not happening in Israel, what else is going on there? Remember that Jesus warned against false prophets in the last days with their mistaken predictions concerning His coming. Could all the attention showered upon unbelieving Israel be a smoke screen of the enemy to divert sincere Christians from the real issues concerning Christ's coming?

Are we being set up for a huge deception?

Chapter 8

GOD'S FORGOTTEN SIGN

H attie's in trouble.
So what else is new?

But this time she's really bad off. Nicolae, the antichrist, father of her illegitimate unborn child, has banished her to a remote Global Community outpost in Colorado. Pregnant, friendless, desperate, she phones Rayford Steele and begs him to come rescue her.

This puts Rayford in a dilemma. He wants to liberate Hattie, but at the risk of his life? And even if he manages to get Hattie safely to the Trib Force's hidden headquarters, could they trust her not to betray their location?

His worst fear: What if this is really a trap set by Nicolae, with Hattie as his bait?

Rayford and Albie discuss it and decide to risk it together. Pretending to be Global Community officers, they boldly show up at the facility. In the office of the director, Pinkerton Stevens, they claim to have orders for moving Hattie out of there.

Surprisingly, Stevens is happy to cooperate. Then he shocks them by identifying himself as a fellow secret believer.

How does Pinkerton Stevens recognize Rayford and Albie as brothers in Christ? By a mark that God mysteriously places on the foreheads of saints during the Great Tribulation, which is invisible to nonbelievers. (Pinkerton had his mark covered, so Rayford and Albie couldn't immediately identify him as a fellow believer.) Chloe has the mark of God too. So do Buck, Chaim, Tsion, and the rest of the Tribulation saints. Even the rescued Hattie finally gets hers as she too becomes a believer.

This mark or seal of God, which believers see on each other, appears at first to be a smudge. Upon closer examination, it turns out to be some kind of a hologram tattoo.

The Bible *does* teach that God will seal His saints in the last days, but is the *Left Behind* interpretation correct? Or once again, do we see here creative fiction?

The core question: Is God's seal literal and visible—or symbolic and therefore unseen?

Let's go to the Bible, our touchstone for truth, and find out.

God's Seal of Obedience

Long ago God spoke through the prophet Isaiah: "Seal the law among my disciples" (Isaiah 8:16). So the seal of God involves compliance with God's commandments. But doesn't lawkeeping signify legalism? Not if first we become disciples through accepting by faith God's forgiving grace. Then comes His call to life-changing obedience: "Do not be conformed to this world, but be transformed by the renewing of your mind" (Romans 12:2).

This renewing of the mind involves a new attitude of cooperation with God's will so that we honor His commandments rather than ignoring or resisting them.

And so the purpose and promise of the new covenant are fulfilled, as we saw in chapter 7 (Hebrews 10:16, 17). Now we can say with King David the psalmist: "I delight to do Your will, O my God, and Your law is within my heart" (Psalm 40:8). Of course, we still suffer with temptations and failure—David certainly did—but our basic attitude now is different, evidenced by its agreement with God's commandments.

Unfortunately, some who claim to be Christians want Jesus only as Savior, not as Leader and Lord. They welcome the privileges but not the responsibilities of belonging to God's family. Sure, they're happy to go to heaven. Amen! But they want to get there on their own terms, flirting with sin while supposing that Jesus has saved them. The New Testament warns against such false faith: "By this we know that we know Him, if we keep His commandments. He who says, 'I know Him,' and does not keep His commandments, is a liar, and the truth is not in him" (1 John 2:3, 4).

Strong warning! But isn't love the only thing God really cares about? Yes, but "love is the fulfillment of the law" (Romans 13:10). Jesus calls us to love God with all our heart and our neighbors as ourselves, and "on these two commandments hang all the Law and the Prophets" (Matthew 22:40). Love for God means keeping the first four commandments; love for neighbor, the last six.

Consider James and Jessica, a young couple in love. They don't mind doing favors for each other, even going out of their way to fulfill each other's wishes. So it is with obedience for true believers: "This is the love of God, that we keep His commandments. And His commandments are not burdensome" (1 John 5:3). We can talk all day about how much we love God, but the real test is obedience to His commandments.

Superficial saints see God as a celestial sugar daddy who supplies everything we want, as long as we ask in faith. This "name-it-and-claim-it" gospel has cheapened the church. Certainly God wants to bless us, but like any caring parent, He gives not necessarily what feels good but what *is* good. Think of Mommy taking a reluctant little boy to the dentist.

But too many simply want a feel-good faith. They want God to bless whatever they are doing instead of doing whatever He is blessing. Perhaps it's easier to agitate politicians to post the Ten Commandments in courtrooms and classrooms than it is to actually obey those same commandments on a personal level. Isn't it ironic that many Christians have urged the posting of the Ten Commandments in certain public places when so many of these same individuals insist that because Christians are not under law but under grace it is heretical to suggest that Christians should keep the commandments?

Have you read them lately? Here they are.

God's Ten Commandments

1. "You shall have no other gods before Me.

2. "You shall not make for yourself a carved image—any likeness of anything that is in heaven above, or that is in the earth beneath, or that is in the water under the earth; you shall not bow down to them nor serve them. For I, the Lord your God, am a jealous God, visiting the iniquity of the fathers upon the children to the third and fourth generations of those who hate Me, but showing mercy to thousands, to those who love Me and keep My commandments.

3. "You shall not take the name of the Lord your God in vain, for the Lord will not hold him guiltless who takes His name in vain.

4. "Remember the Sabbath day, to keep it holy. Six days you shall labor and do all your work, but the seventh day is the Sabbath of the Lord your God. In it you shall do no work: you, nor your son, nor your daughter, nor your male servant, nor your female servant, nor your cattle, nor your stranger who is within your gates. For in six days the Lord made the heavens and the earth, the sea, and all that is in them, and rested the seventh day. Therefore the Lord blessed the Sabbath day and hallowed it.

5. "Honor your father and your mother, that your days may be long upon the land which the Lord your God is giving you.

6. "You shall not murder.

7. "You shall not commit adultery.

8. "You shall not steal.

9. "You shall not bear false witness against your neighbor.

10. "You shall not covet your neighbor's house; you shall not covet your neighbor's wife, nor his male servant, nor his female servant, nor his ox, nor his donkey, nor anything that is your neighbor's" (Exodus 20:3-17).

So there we have them: 10 simple and powerful expressions of God's will for our lives. Satan hates the Ten Commandments because they confront the anarchy and disobedience that destroy society and individuals. His delusion that the New Testament has abolished or diminished God's law has deeply damaged the Christian community.

Consider the seventh commandment, forbidding adultery. We don't seem to take it seriously anymore. Extramarital affairs are commonly portrayed on TV and in movies.

And what about the fourth commandment? God

says "Remember the Sabbath." Evidently He knew it would be forgotten. The devil has aimed some of his sharpest arrows at the Sabbath, and why not, since it establishes God as our Creator? Through our neglect of God's appointed weekly memorial of Creation, atheism and Darwinism have spread their poison.

There's more. Have you ever explored the fascinating background of the Sabbath?

Culmination of Creation

Come with me long ago and far away to the Garden of Eden. Everything was beautiful and peaceful. Lush green meadows sparkled with wildflowers. Rivers raced through fragrant forests and descended through waterfalls. Exotic birds of all colors frolicked among the trees, their songs a chorus of praise. Then God created a beautiful woman as His crowning masterpiece and presented her to Adam. He gave them together the custody of their Paradise garden home.

As the sun was about to set on the sixth day of Creation Week, God looked around and nodded approvingly. Everything was good, as perfect as He Himself could make it.

What happened next? "Then God blessed the seventh day and sanctified it, because in it He rested from all His work which God had created and made" (Genesis 2:3). This word "sanctified" is just like its cousin word "saint," meaning "set apart for God." (Some Bible versions translate the word as "holy." "Holy" and "sanctified" mean the same thing—that which is dedicated exclusively to God.)

So God set apart the seventh day for rest. Not that He was tired! He sanctified the Sabbath for us to celebrate His accomplishment with Him. Adam and Eve had done nothing themselves to earn the right to rest, yet God invited them to share the joy of His creation.

You may know that Jesus Christ actually implemented the creation of the world. (See John 1 and Hebrews 1.) So the Sabbath has special meaning for Christians. In fact, Sabbath rest in Christ's finished work symbolizes what Christianity stands for. Other world religions typically focus upon self-improvement, what people can do to better themselves, but Christianity celebrates Christ's accomplishments on our behalf. That's why the Sabbath points us away from ourselves, away from our works, to trust in what Jesus has done for us.

The Sabbath also provides rich insight into the meaning of Calvary. Let's reverently visit the cross on that fatal Friday afternoon. How things have changed since that first Friday of Creation Week! In place of beautiful meadows and forests, we see the bare rocks of Golgotha, the "place of the skull." Instead of the happy songs of Paradise birds, we hear the mocking shout: "Crucify Him!"

Yes, so much has changed. But one thing remains the same between those two Friday afternoons. Once again Jesus completes a work for humanity. With His dying breath He cries: "It is finished!" (John 19:30). Mission accomplished! A hostage world now redeemed!

Then as the sun begins to set, friends of Jesus lay Him to rest inside a tomb. There He remains over Sabbath hours. We can now recognize it as a memorial of His completed work for our salvation—His Sabbath rest. After His quiet Sabbath repose, Jesus arises and ascends to heaven's royal throne.

Do you see it? The Sabbath memorializes Christ's two greatest accomplishments—creating us and saving us, giving us life and then new life. These are the reasons above all others that God is worthy of our worship. (See Revelation 4:11; 5:9.) No wonder Scripture declares the Sabbath to be the special sign, or seal, between God and His people: "Keep my Sabbaths holy, that they may be a sign between us. Then you will know that I am the Lord your God" (Ezekiel 20:20, NIV).

So God says: "I created you and I saved you. Remember this every week by setting apart the seventh day for Me, even as I have set it apart for you. It is the special sign or seal of the covenant between us."

The Bible never says, as we sometimes do, that just any day of the week can serve as the Sabbath. God specifically appointed the seventh day to memorialize both creation and salvation. It's similar to your anniversary or birthday—the commemoration of a changeless, historic event. No other day could ever fit.

Can you see how precious is the Sabbath to every believer? God knew we needed its provision of rest from our duties and burdens. Often we hurry through the week, out of time and out of touch with God and with each other. The Sabbath is God's invitation to take an entire day apart from life's responsibilities to enjoy His creative and redemptive accomplishments with Him and with fellow believers. And beyond the benefits of rest and refreshment, we express faith in Him as our Maker and Redeemer by entering His Sabbath rest.

Symbol of Salvation

Let's explore deeper into the Sabbath as a symbol of salvation. God's law demands that all our work be faithfully performed and finished: "Six days shalt thou labour and do all thy work" (Exodus 20:9, KJV). And so we work hard all week as we try to accomplish our tasks. But then the end of the week comes, and guess what! The work is not done. When the sun goes down each Friday afternoon—even after a long week of effort—we have to confess our unfinished business. The bills aren't all paid. The garage isn't cleaned out. The garden isn't weeded.

So what should you do?

God invites us, although we are undeserving, to rest anyway—not because we have finished our work but because He has finished His work and earned the right to rest. This is the core meaning of the Sabbath. We turn our attention away from our inadequate works and identify ourselves with His perfect work. And so, right there among all the duties required by the Ten Commandments, God offers us rest from our unfinished works by reminding us of His perfect work on our behalf.

The implications of this go far deeper than cooking and cleaning and bill paying. When it comes to our works for salvation, we trust not in our own works but in Christ's works! The devil has deceived many dedicated people to trust in their own works for salvation. No wonder he hates Sabbath rest. Week by week the Sabbath assures believers that despite shortcomings, we stand complete in Christ. What tremendous therapy for legalism! Finally we have relief from those awful feelings about not being good enough. There's no need now to worry about penance or working our way back into God's favor. This is the powerful message of the Sabbath.

As our Creator and Savior, Jesus proclaimed Himself "Lord of the Sabbath" (Matthew 12:8, NIV). He kept the Sabbath holy all His life, and He never taught that the day which memorializes His work should be forgotten or changed.

The Seal of God

Let's recap what we've seen in this chapter.

- Bible truth is plain and clear. We don't need to

speculate about holograms or tattoos.

- God will seal His law within faithful disciples.

- His Spirit accomplishes this through the new covenant promise in which God's law is written upon transformed minds and hearts.

- The Sabbath memorializes creation and salvation—life and new life—which are the main reasons we worship God.

- Thus Sabbath rest in Christ is the sign or seal between God and His people, signified not by a literal smudge on one's skin but by willingly setting apart the seventh day for Him.

How did Sunday come to replace the Sabbath? It's a sad yet intriguing story of Bible truth becoming corrupted with legalism and mingled with pagan sun worship.

Turn the page, and we'll see how and when this happened.

Chapter 9

ATTACK FROM BABYLON

I t was party time at the palace in Babylon.
Fine wine flowed like rainwater gushing down a
gutter. Sultry women lounged everywhere, the most
beautiful in the world, eager to indulge every carnal plea-
sure of the thousand princes present. Raucous sounds of
music and dancing echoed through the banquet hall,
mingling with the bellowing of drunken celebrants.

Then the festivities plunged into blasphemy. The
king of Babylon praised the power of his pagan gods
and mocked the apparently helpless God of heaven.
He shouted for his servants to fetch the gold and sil-
ver chalices captured from Jerusalem's Temple. He
poured wine into them for his princes, and together
they toasted their abomination.

The world had never seen a party quite like this
one. But God was watching. Just when the feverish
merrymaking reached its climax, the celebration
abruptly stopped. Lustful hollering ceased as princes
howled in terror. Women screamed and hid under
tables. The king dropped his golden goblet, splash-
ing its contents on his robes. His knees quaked.

What was happening?

The omnipresent and omnipotent God in heaven decided that the Babylonians had crossed a line. It was time to call them to account for their blasphemies. A huge superhuman hand appeared from nowhere and burned these words of doom into the palace wall: "Mene, mene, tekel upharsin," which translated means: "God has numbered your kingdom, and finished it." "You have been weighed in the balances, and found wanting" (Daniel 5:25-27).

Weighed and wanting! This decree of divine judgment doomed Babylon.

Enemy soldiers waving swords stormed into the palace and slaughtered King Belshazzar. The party was over. Babylon was out of business.

Identifying Babylon

The event dramatized above really happened, 2,500 years ago. You can read it in your Bible, Daniel 5. The sentence on Babylon was final: "'I will punish the king of Babylon and that nation,' declares the Lord, 'for their iniquity, and the land of the Chaldeans; and I will make it an everlasting desolation'" (Jeremiah 25:12, NASB). Indeed, Babylon has lain desolate all these years. Attempts to restore the ancient site have stalled and failed. Presently Saddam Hussein is trying to restore it as a national historical monument, but not as a metropolitan complex.

The *Left Behind* books say much about Babylon. But we must be careful, since *Left Behind* is self-described as "an end-of-time fiction series." Fiction has its place, but when it comes to our eternal destiny, nothing substitutes for solid Bible truth. So what does the Bible say about Babylon in the last days? Will it be a real city? Or does it symbolize something else?

The answer is obvious from the book of Revelation. End-time Babylon is "the mother of harlots and of the abominations of the earth" (Revelation 17:5). A city can't literally become a mother! So the city of Babylon must be symbolic. Well, a city is where people congregate. Babylon is the worldwide mother of the congregation of the antichrist who rebels against God's covenant and His commandments. This is the picture of Babylon that emerges from studying Scripture and its historical background.

Babylon's roots reach way back to the ancient city of Babel, whose citizens rebelled against God. Following Noah's flood they built a tower designed to reach "to the heavens" (Genesis 11:4, NIV), no doubt because they feared another flood. Thus they disbelieved God's promise that such a thing would never again happen. In seeking to save themselves by their own devices and accomplishments, Babel defied God's will.

Centuries later King Nebuchadnezzar of the Neo-Babylon Empire invaded Jerusalem and destroyed the Temple, taking captive God's people. God warned King Nebuchadnezzar in a dream not to become proud over his accomplishments. But the king defiantly boasted, "Is not this the great Babylon I have built as the royal residence, by my mighty power and for the glory of my majesty?" (Daniel 4:30, NIV). God promptly stripped the haughty king of his royal authority and taught him his lesson.

Babylon's last ruler, Belshazzar, empowered to rule by his father King Nabonidus, maintained its heritage of self-exaltation and rejection of God's grace until his follies proved fatal, as we have seen.

Although the literal city of Babylon remains unpopulated, its tradition of rejecting God's covenant lives on today. Babylon throughout Scripture is a symbol for rebellion, confusion, and self-sufficiency, which explains its spiritual rather than literal meaning for the last days. And Babylon does not represent an alien attack upon Christianity from outside the church. Rather, it signifies fallen, apostate Christianity—with true believers still trapped inside its deceptions and false doctrines. Because God loves them, He calls them to come out (Revelation 18:4).

Back in Old Testament times, the return of the Hebrew people to the literal land of the covenant meant coming out physically from geographical Babylon. Today the act is symbolic, meaning that God's people will be liberated from the false doctrines of spiritual Babylon and come to Jesus, their intercessor in Heaven. "You have come to . . . the heavenly Jerusalem, . . . to Jesus the Mediator of the new covenant" (Hebrews 12:22-24).

The Protestant Reformers all recognized that Babylon now symbolizes a church fallen from faithfulness. No surprise there. We've noticed again and again how God's people throughout history wandered from His will. All this was predicted, of course. (Recall 2 Peter 2:1, 2; Acts 20:29, 30.) We've mentioned that various pagan rites and ceremonies that Christ and the apostles never heard of infiltrated Christianity early in its history. Finally the church itself became an anti-Christian power. The apostles would never have recognized it! In chapter 4 of this book we noticed the prophecy of Daniel 7, which specifies the world kingdoms that in succeeding centuries would oppose God's people (literal and spiritual) and His truth, extending from Babylon to Rome. In this chapter we'll explore what type of profane religion those empires had in common.

Worshiping the Sun

Adoration of the sun can be traced all the way

back to near Noah's time. Nimrod, his great-grand-son, became a "mighty one on the earth" (Genesis 10:8). Beginning with his Tower of Babel, Nimrod's achievements adorn the records and legends of ancient history. But this talented leader was evil, a father of counterfeit worship.

False worship also thrived through Ishtar, called the queen of heaven, goddess of love and fertility. Ishtar, according to legend, birthed a son, Tammuz, without a father. So here in pagan worship long before Christ we find the virgin birth counterfeited!

Worship of the sun god Shamash from ancient Sumeria, a predecessor of Babylon, spread throughout Mesopotamia via Assyria and then Babylon. The major Babylonian god, Marduk, was sometimes identified as the sun and could be depicted with sun waves emanating from his shoulders. The early Babylonian king Hammurabi claimed to have received his famous law code from Shamash (*The Encyclopedia of Religion,* vol. 14, p. 136). A temple to the sun was erected in Babylon, and it was known as "the house of the judge of the world" *(ibid.).*

The Persians, according to the ancient historian Herodotus, offered sacrifices to the sun *(ibid.,* p. 137). Their god Mithra absorbed the name of Shamash once the Persians had conquered Babylon in 539 B.C. (Remember the story of this conquest told earlier?)

In Greece the sun god was Helios and was often pictured in Grecian art as a god riding in a chariot pulled by powerful steeds *(ibid.).* The Island of Rhodes was very deep into sun worship. In fact, the Colossus of Rhodes, one of the seven wonders of the ancient world, was a statue of the sun god. Apollo was another Greek god that seems to have been tied closely to sun worship.

In ancient Rome itself sun worship at first was

pretty much a rarity (*ibid.,* p. 138). However, relatively late in the history of the empire—in A.D. 274, slightly more than a couple of centuries after Jesus' birth, death, resurrection, and ascension—Emperor Aurelias established the worship of Sol Invictus ("the invincible sun"). He was the very first emperor to wear a diadem, which symbolized the sun. Rome celebrated the birthday of the sun on—are you ready?—December 25! Eighty years later Pope Liberius declared that December 25 was the time that Christians should celebrate the Feast of the Nativity—Christmas (*ibid.,* p. 139).

Why worship the sun? Well, the sun brings light, warmth, growth—all needed for life itself. Reigning supreme over nature, the bright and glowing sun is a natural object of worship for those who reject or do not know their true Creator.

When God rescued His people from Egypt, He illustrated His omnipotence by overpowering the sun with three days of darkness. All who turned from the sun god (Egypt was a hotbed of sun worship) and put the lamb's blood on their doorpost were saved from death. Nevertheless, Israel exported sun idolatry in the Exodus. The golden calf they reverenced represented Apis, the Egyptian bull god who helped the deceased pharaohs get to the sun.

Throughout Old Testament times adoration of pagan deities hijacked true worship in Israel. King Solomon, the very one who built God's Temple, defiled Jerusalem with sun worship. God's people baked cakes to the queen of heaven (Jeremiah 7:18). And Ezekiel 8 records the revolting scenario of women reverencing Tammuz, an ancient sun god, in the Temple, and men bowing to the sun.

Unbelievable! Pagan worship in Jerusalem's holy

ATTACK FROM BABYLON

Temple! Faithful prophets called Israel away from the sun to their Creator. They pointed to the seventh-day Sabbath, God's weekly reminder of Creation. Yet the Jewish people persisted in paganism. Finally the Lord gave them up to be captives in Babylon, that ancient center of pagan worship.

At last God's people learned their lesson. But they went to the other extreme. After returning to Jerusalem from Babylon, they shunned their pagan neighbors to prevent contamination. By the time of Jesus, the Jews had largely quarantined themselves from the Gentiles around them.

Meanwhile, sun worship thrived in the pagan world. The Romans maintained Babylonian sun worship traditions, naming the days of the week according to their heathen religion. Although the current English names for the days of the week have Anglo-Saxon roots, they reflect Roman influence. On Sunday they reverenced the sun. On Monday the moon. On Tuesday, Mars. On Wednesday, Mercury. On Thursday they honored Jupiter. On Friday, Venus. On Saturday? You guessed it—Saturn. Just as the sun rules over the planets, so Sunday attained preeminence above the other days of the week.

The earliest Christians kept themselves from pagan worship, often suffering intense persecution. Thousands were fed to lions or burned alive. Yet the church survived and thrived.

Then the devil, having failed to overcome Christianity through opposition, switched his strategy. He ingeniously corrupted the church's faith through an insidious blend of legalism and paganism, which go together since righteousness by works is the essence of pagan religion. Little by little he mingled the ceremonies of sun worship with Christian teaching.

Paganism Infiltrates Christianity

Why would the church be drawn to paganism? For one thing, Christians wanted to distance themselves from anything Jewish. Jews, you see, had put themselves in the emperor's doghouse. They despised Roman authority, continually revolting to regain national independence.

The empire struck back. In A.D. 49 Emperor Claudius expelled Jews from Rome for their rioting (Acts 18:2). Things worsened. Strict sanctions were enjoined upon Jews. They responded by refusing to pray for God's blessing on the emperor. To Rome, this was treason.

In A.D. 70 Roman armies besieged Jerusalem. Jewish people were starved, burned, crucified, or otherwise killed. Their fabulous Temple lay in ruins. Anti-Semitic riots resulted in even stronger strictures upon Jews.

Because Christians shared the same background as Jews, Romans typically viewed both groups alike. No fair! Christians desired peace with the emperor, rendering to Caesar his due. Yet they suffered anyway, as if they were Jews—beyond the persecution already theirs for Christ's sake. No wonder Christians divorced themselves from everything Jewish. They sought a new identity more favorable with the empire.

During the decades following Jerusalem's destruction, Christianity became largely Gentile and began looking to Rome as its new church center. This was natural, since Rome was the capital city of the empire. Besides, both Peter and Paul concluded their ministry there. By A.D. 95 Clement, bishop of Rome, had become quite prominent. His epistles commanded respect among believers. Some even judged them inspired.

Rome's influence in the church increased further

after the second destruction of Jerusalem in A.D. 135. Emperor Hadrian outlawed Jewish worship, particularly their Sabbathkeeping. Christians felt compelled to separate themselves completely from their Hebrew heritage, including the Sabbath. Gradually they adapted and substituted in its place pagan customs common in the Roman Empire.

Christians Begin Keeping Sunday

The church put a Christian face on its compromises, of course. We see this in the first definite reference to keeping Sunday, about the year A.D. 135. The Epistle of Barnabas, authored by a respected church leader, argues for abandoning the Sabbath. Barnabas suggests that Sabbathkeeping is impossible in this present world since all believers are imperfect. He asks, How can we have rest until God's work within our hearts is complete? But in heaven, he states, "we shall be able to treat it [the Sabbath] as holy, after we have first been made holy ourselves" (translation by E. Goodspeed, pp. 40, 41; quoted by Samuele Bacchiocchi, *From Sabbath to Sunday* [Rome: The Pontifical Gregorian University Press, 1977], p. 221).

How sad! Barnabas had forgotten that the Sabbath invites imperfect people to rest in Christ's perfect accomplishments. If early Christians had retained the pure gospel, they never would have forsaken Sabbath rest.

But as it was, the church sank into a fatal mixture of legalism and paganism. Believers ready to sacrifice life itself rather than yield their commitment to Christ allowed their faith to be corrupted, adopting false teachings that suffocated the gospel of God's grace. Although many Christians refused to compromise gospel truth, the church in general suffered a serious loss of faith. Pagan symbols and ceremonies slithered in quietly. Heathen holidays became Christian holy days.

Think about it. What do Easter eggs and bunny rabbits have to do with the resurrection of Christ? Nothing really. They were pagan fertility symbols. The church adopted them to celebrate new birth in Jesus. The *Encyclopedia Britannica* states "Christianity . . . incorporated in its celebration of the great Christian feast day [Easter] many of the heathen rites and customs . . . of the spring festival" (1961 ed., vol. 7, p. 859, "Easter").

The newer edition pretty much says the same thing: "Around the Christian observance of Easter . . . folk customs have collected, many of which have been handed down from the ancient ceremonial and symbolism of European and Middle Eastern pagan spring festivals brought into relation with the resurrection theme" (*Encyclopaedia Britannica,* Micropaedia, vol. 4, p. 333). And *The Encyclopedia American* agrees (vol. 9, p. 561).

Other heathen feasts infiltrated the church. For centuries pagans had celebrated the birth of Tammuz on December 25. You've heard of that date. Now there's nothing morally wrong with exchanging gifts at Christmas, although it's not the real date of Christ's birth. And the Easter bunny may not be worth worrying about. But here's the question. Since our Christian holidays come from sun worship, how do we know that other areas of our worship, perhaps something really important, weren't tampered with too?

Scholars today recognize the pagan roots in Christianity. Roman Catholic Cardinal John Henry Newman relates in his book *The Development of the Christian Religion:* "Temples, incense, oil lamps, votive offerings, holy water, holidays and seasons of devotion, processions, blessing of fields, sacerdotal vestments, the tonsure, and images . . . are all of pagan origin" (p. 359).

Startling, isn't it?

Gradually and without fanfare, Christians adopted and adapted the rituals of paganism, especially regarding sun worship. Not that they actually worshiped the sun. They were celebrating Christ's birth and resurrection. Even so, they assimilated the pagan ceremonies of those who did worship the sun.

Pagans became comfortable with Christianity. And why not? They could keep celebrating their heathen holidays—now in the name of Jesus. But damage was done. Pure faith lay buried in pagan tradition. Accommodation took the place of transformation.

By the fourth century, Christianity so reflected paganism that the emperor found it convenient to become a believer. Constantine the Great proclaimed himself a convert in the year 312. (Some people question the sincerity of his conversion.) Persecution ceased. Outright pagan sacrifices were outlawed. Christian worship became official.

Delighted church leaders endorsed the new Christian regime. Working together, church and state mixed faith in Christ with sun worship rituals. On March 7, 321, Constantine ordered his empire to respect the "venerable day of the sun." Not the Son of God, but the sun—the day of pagan sun worship.

Suffocating the Sabbath

For centuries Christians kept both the seventh-day Sabbath and the weekly day of sun worship. Slowly, however, the first day of the week gained more and more prominence, particularly with Constantine's promotion. The cities of Rome and Alexandria led the way in substituting Sunday for the

Bible Sabbath, Saturday.

As the centuries rolled on, the day of the sun increased in importance to the church. In 538 a council at Orléans, France, forbade all work on the first day of the week. Eventually laws became so strict a woman could be sentenced to seven days' penance for washing her hair on Sunday.

Thus Sunday overcame the Sabbath. Nevertheless, quite a few Christians still worshiped on the seventh day. Many kept both days holy. Pockets of Sabbathkeepers remained in areas known now as Egypt, Tunisia, Turkey, Palestine, and Syria. Also in Ethiopia, Armenia, and Yugoslavia. Even in Ireland. Some evidence suggests that Saint Patrick in the British Isles kept the seventh day holy. But after he died, the Irish church ceased resisting Rome, and Sabbathkeeping faded. Finally Sunday eclipsed the Sabbath, although even then traces of Sabbathkeeping remained here and there.

Those who honored the Bible Sabbath found themselves endangered. Anyone who accepted the Bible as the only rule of faith and who insisted upon Jesus alone as intercessor qualified as a heretic. The burning of heretics began at Orléans, France, in the eleventh century. Persecution intensified during the Crusades. Then came the notorious Inquisition. Thousands lost their lives for their faith.

How could Christians wage war against brothers and sisters in Christ? Church leaders believed that killing heretics saved thousands of others from following them into eternal torment. Even the heretics themselves might repent when facing the flames. At least that's what church leaders hoped for.

And it wasn't just Rome that persecuted. Protestants also committed horrible atrocities against fellow believers with whom they disagreed, such as the Anabaptists, whose crime was insisting that nobody has the right to choose religion for someone else—not even parents for their babies. This agreed with the scriptural teaching that only those who can believe for themselves should be baptized—by dipping under water rather than sprinkling. (Consider Mark 16:16: "He who believes and is baptized will be saved." The word "baptize" derives from the Greek word meaning "submerge." Sprinkling is another example of pagan customs that crept into the church and were retained by many Protestants.)

In gruesome parody, some Protestants even drowned men and women who dared to be rebaptized. (For example, followers of the Swiss Reformer Ulrich Zwingli drowned Anabaptist leader Felix Manz during a persecution campaign in 1527.)

Protestants also persecuted Catholics in territories under their control more frequently than many realize today.

Though disturbed by all their intolerance, we need not question the motives of our ancestors. Instead, we can pray with our Savior: "Father, forgive them, for they know not what they do." Let's remember the good done by the church. Monasteries maintained hospitals and cared for orphans, widows, and the sick. And all of us owe appreciation to the Roman Catholic Church for faithfully preserving the Scriptures through the painstaking efforts of faithful monks who copied the Bible word by word.

Unfortunately, Bibles were chained to monastery walls. Laypeople had to learn secondhand from the clergy, sworn to uphold Rome's traditions. Of course, most commoners could not read at this time. Knowledge of the Scriptures became scarce. The

Christian church had descended into medieval darkness, full of legalism and confusion. A reformation was desperately needed.

God brought Martin Luther and others to the rescue in the sixteenth century. Emerging from more than a millennium of spiritual confusion in Christianity, these pioneers of the Reformation were not without serious error. Regrettably, Luther, for example, produced his famous anti-Jewish diatribes and agreed with persecuting Anabaptists. Even so, he and his fellow Reformers made important advances in restoring the fundamentals of the New Testament. Facing fierce opposition from Rome on account of the gospel, they identified the established church system as Babylon of prophecy. This insight came from their study of the book of Revelation. Daniel in the Old Testament also held special interest, notably chapter 7, as we have seen. But the Reformers missed something fascinating in verse 25 relating to the antichrist power in years gone by: "He shall think to change times and laws" (KJV)—or literally, "times in the law."

Changing the Sabbath Day

Has the church tried to change the Ten Commandments, specifically concerning time? Yes. In fact, it became official Catholic church policy.

Around the year 1400 Petrus de Ancharano asserted that "the pope can modify divine law, since his power is not of man, but of God, and he acts in the place of God on earth" (Lucius Ferraris, "Papa, II," in *Prompta Bibliotheca* [Venice: Caspa Storti, 1772], cited by C. Mervyn Maxwell, *God Cares,* vol. 1, 128.)

Martin Luther denounced this teaching of the church. In his famous debate with papal representative Johann Eck, he declared that no church tradition would rule his life. Only the Holy Scriptures could control his conscience.

But Eck had an ace up his sleeve. He called Luther to account for keeping Sunday in place of the Bible Sabbath. Here is his challenge to the great Reformer. "Scripture teaches: 'Remember to hallow the Sabbath day; six days shall you labor and do all your work, but the seventh day is the Sabbath day of the Lord your God,' etc. Yet the *church* has changed the Sabbath into Sunday on its own authority, on which *you have no Scripture*" (Johann Eck, *Enchiridion of Commonplaces of John Eck Against Luther and Other Enemies of the Church,* trans. F. L. Battles, 2d ed. [Grand Rapids: Calvin Theological Seminary, 1978], vol. 8, p. 13, cited by Maxwell, *God Cares,* vol. 1, p. 128).

Eck had a point Luther could not deny. In his battle against church tradition, the Reformer had not yet come to terms with the Sabbath question. He had his hands full merely reestablishing the basics of Christianity.

The Catholic Church today acknowledges the origin of Sundaykeeping. This eye-opening quote is from *The Convert's Catechism of Catholic Doctrine:*

"Q. Which is the Sabbath day?

"A. Saturday is the Sabbath day.

"Q. Why do we observe Sunday instead of Saturday.

"A. We observe Sunday instead of Saturday because the Catholic Church transferred the solemnity from Saturday to Sunday" (Peter Geiermann, *The Convert's Catechism of Catholic Doctrine* [Rockford, Ill: Tan Books, 1977], p. 50).

Fascinating. We also read in a much-respected book, *The Faith of Millions:* "Since Saturday, not Sunday, is specified in the Bible, isn't it curious that non-Catholics who profess to take their religion directly from the Bible and not from the Church, observe Sunday instead of Saturday? . . . That observance remains as a reminder of the Mother Church from which the non-Catholic sects broke away—like a boy running away from home but still carrying in his pocket a picture of his mother or a lock of her hair" (John A. O'Brien, *The Faith of Millions,* rev. ed. [Huntington, Ind: Our Sunday Visitor, 1974], pp. 400, 401).

Perhaps Protestants ought to ask themselves why they keep Sunday, since tradition provided its origin. They also might notice the mention of "Mother Church" in light of the Reformers' own warning about Babylon. You see, Scripture teaches that in earth's final days Babylon would have daughters—other groups that maintain and promote Rome's non-biblical teachings and traditions, thus betraying the Reformation (Revelation 17:5).

True Sheep Follow
the True Shepherd

What shall we do with what we've seen in this chapter? It's easy to depend upon friends or trusted leaders to tell us what to do. But if Christ really is Lord in our lives, will we not follow Him instead of pagan-based traditions or our own religious preferences?

Jesus Himself said it best: "My sheep hear My voice, and I know them, and they follow Me" (John 10:27).

Let's not get left behind as truth goes marching on!

Chapter 10

PERSECUTING PATRIOTS

Pity the poor president of the United States. Gerald Fitzhugh is one of the most frustrated, pathetic personalities in *Left Behind*'s stable of fictional characters. Antichrist Nicolae Carpathia outwits, outmaneuvers, and outclasses him at every turn in seizing control of the world.

First Nicolae weasels the president out of his new jet, *Air Force One*. Then he takes control of America's military resources, making Fitzhugh the puppet head of the committee to disarm the world—while stocking Carpathia's arsenal. The crafty antichrist eventually robs the president even of his country as America is swallowed up by the United Nations, renamed the Global Community, with headquarters in New Babylon. American sovereignty is forfeited, its territory combined with Canada and Mexico as just another one of 10 regions in Nicolae's world kingdom.

Here we have one of the most puzzling aspects of the *Left Behind* scenario—the omission of any role in final events for the United States as a nation. Yet in so many ways America is the world's superpower: politically, financially, militarily, culturally, technologically, and so on.

111

The whole planet is addicted to Hollywood movies and telecasts. Wall Street sneezes, and global financial markets catch a cold. In the Middle East both Israelis and Arabs invoke America's mediation. War in the Balkans, though on European territory, requires American involvement. Even the United Nations would have little influence without America's participation.

Whether people like it or not, the United States is undeniably important to the world. You can love America or hate it, but you can't ignore its stature among the nations of the world. Yet the *Left Behind* series does exactly that.

Does Bible prophecy portray America as a nation that loses its superpower sovereignty? No way. The United States will play a leading role in final events. This is not necessarily a good thing, as we will see in this chapter. Scripture foretold both the religious freedom we enjoy and also the impending loss of it.

America in Prophecy

Where do we find the United States symbolized? Right in the heart of the last book of the Bible, Revelation. "Then I saw another beast coming up out of the earth, and he had two horns like a lamb and spoke like a dragon" (Revelation 13:11).

How should we interpret this?

A beast in Bible prophecy, you may recall, represents a kingdom or government (Daniel 7:17, 23). The government represented here differs from others in several ways. Previous kingdoms in Daniel and Revelation arise out of the water, which represents the chaos of "peoples, multitudes, nations" (Revelation 17:15)—a fitting symbol for the military hordes of Egypt, Assyria, and Babylon as well as the

PERSECUTING PATRIOTS

crowded Old World of Europe and the Middle East. This new nation, however, springs up from the earth. Also, this new government doesn't have crowns like the others, so it's not a monarchy. Instead, it has a gentle government with two horns like a lamb. (Horns in the ancient Near East and in Scripture symbolize power—typically political or imperial power.)

Does this symbolize the miracle of American government, a democratic republic free from entanglements with an official state church? Recall that colonial governments in the New World were intolerant church-state coalitions. In view of that, it is truly amazing that when Americans drew up their Constitution they included a Bill of Rights and guaranteed religious freedom with its First Amendment.

A genuine miracle, this new form of government! The church-state coalition of the medieval times violated Christ's instruction to keep separate what belongs to Caesar (the government) from what belongs to God (Matthew 22:21).

Government must protect the free exercise of religion but not promote or establish any particular belief system. And this is what the prophecy called for: A different form of government with two lamblike horns—the peaceful separation of the powers of church and state. And this new type of nation would emerge in a new world. What else could this be than the United States in prophecy?

How exciting! But then we notice that this gentle lamblike government suddenly reverses course and speaks with dragonlike voice (Revelation 13:11). The book of Revelation itself identifies the dragon as Satan (Revelation 12:3, 9). A nation speaks through its laws. Does this mean that America will pass legislation that will deny its democratic principles? Will it revert to

113

DDD-5

the coercive ways of the Puritans, reflecting methods carried over from the medieval church?

Unfortunately, some unusual and distressing events will occur in the United States. We find this in Revelation 13:12-14: "And he exercises all the authority of the first beast in his presence, and causes the earth and those who dwell in it to worship the first beast, whose deadly wound was healed. He performs great signs, so that he even makes fire come down from heaven on the earth in the sight of men. And he deceives those who dwell on the earth by those signs which he was granted to do in the sight of the beast, telling those who dwell on the earth to make an image to the beast who was wounded by the sword and lived."

By miracles counterfeiting God's power, America will lead the world to form an image to the ancient Holy Roman Empire. What could this mean? An image is a replica or copy of the original. The Old World power was a union of church and state, a religious system wedded to government and supported by law. This New World image to the Holy Roman Empire, being a copy of that system, must also be a union of church and state that would behave like a dragon. In other words, America will forfeit its principles of religious freedom and begin a persecution.

Incredible? Indeed. But who would expect a lamb to speak like a satanic dragon? Bible symbolism indicates that America will have a drastic change in its attitude toward religious freedom. And notice that this nation has world-changing influence, "telling those who dwell on the earth" (verse 14) to reflect these principles. In our world today, only the United States has such influence. So, according to the Bible, America's power over nations will increase—not decrease—as the end of the world approaches.

What could motivate America to commit itself to coercion and intolerance? Perhaps some national emergency. History shows that people in crisis willingly trade liberty for security. In our next chapter we will depict a potential scenario for Armageddon, in which the antichrist's deceptions and persecutions will challenge the faith of God's commandment-keeping remnant.

The Threat of Emergency Powers

Most Americans are so accustomed to freedom that they cannot conceive of anything else from their government. But at crucial times throughout American history, presidents have restricted liberty by activating their little-known but extremely powerful emergency provisions.

In the nineteenth century the great emancipator, Abraham Lincoln, implemented these presidential war powers during the superheated hostilities of the Civil War. Lincoln, who exercised his war powers to proclaim the freedom of slaves, ironically used that same authority to impair the civil rights of others for the sake of national security. Lincoln regarded spying, sabotage, recruiting for the enemy, and other threats so grave that he resorted to military arrests of civilians and the suspension of rights to a fair trial and to the appeals process.

Badgered by scattered criticism, Lincoln explained: "I felt that measures otherwise unconstitutional might become lawful by becoming indispensable to the preservation of the Constitution through the preservation of the nation" (Winfred A. Harbison and Alfred H. Kelly, *The American Constitution* [New York: W. W. Norton, 1963], p. 435). And so America's patron saint of freedom became a dictator for the sake of national security.

During the past century such a triumph of executive war powers over the Bill of Rights became legal in 1917 when the United States plunged into World War I. That June the Wilson administration prodded Congress to pass the Lever Food Control Bill, which authorized the government to mobilize against food shortages and escalating prices. The bill was so broad as to subjugate virtually the entire national economy under any regulation the president considered necessary to vanquish the Germans.

When Hitler's rising sun launched another war, followed by Japan's blitzkrieg on Pearl Harbor, Roosevelt expanded the emergency powers of his presidency. Congress and the courts complied. (Roosevelt's programs enjoyed much smoother sailing through Congress than Lincoln's had in 1861 or Wilson's in 1917. Lower courts declined to challenge the ever-expanding federal war powers, and the Supreme Court habitually refused to overturn or even review their decisions.)

One of the darkest chapters in the history of the Supreme Court was leaving unchecked Roosevelt's imprisonment of more than 100,000 Japanese Americans, 70 percent of whom were American citizens. Arresting them at their homes and jobs, the government shipped them to detention camps for up to four years of imprisonment. Amazingly, "no more than twelve openly resisted, and four of these cases eventually reached the U.S. Supreme Court" (Samuel Walker, *In Defense of American Liberties: a History of the ACLU* [New York: Oxford University Press, 1990], p. 138).

Public opinion and the media let it happen, while the Supreme Court sustained the government's detention policies.

PERSECUTING PATRIOTS

Evidently you can't count on the Court in a national emergency. Nor can you count on the Congress, the president, the media, or your local police. Even your best friends can't save you. You can count only on God. Meanwhile, the radical emergency powers of the U.S. government are still there and ready to be enforced.

America's History of Persecution

If persecution in America still seems impossible, consider its history. Ironically, many settlers seeking religious freedom were unwilling to extend that same liberty to others. The Puritans crossed the Atlantic escaping persecution from the Church of England, settling what is now Massachusetts. You would think they would have been happy to enjoy their freedom and let others do the same. But no. When William Penn's band of Quakers sailed past the colony of Massachusetts, they nearly fell prey to a band of Christian pirates.

Note this order from Cotton Mather, the famous Puritan clergyman: "There be now at sea a ship called 'Welcome,' which has on board one hundred or more of the heretics and malignants called Quakers. . . . The General Court has given sacred orders to . . . waylay the said 'Welcome' . . . and make captive the said Penn and his ungodly crew, so that the Lord may be glorified and not mocked with the heathen worship of these people. . . . We shall not only do the Lord great good by punishing the wicked, but we shall make great good for His ministers and people. Yours in the bowels of Christ, Cotton Mather."

Captivated by love for God! A new dimension to Christian compassion!

Providentially, the preacher's persecuting pirates failed. Penn's Quakers landed safely and settled the area that later came to be known as Pennsylvania.

The Puritans tyrannized not only outsiders but also their own. They spied a sea captain kissing his wife on Sunday and locked him in the stocks. The poor guy probably hadn't seen her for months. Another unfortunate fellow fell into a pond and skipped Sunday services to dry his suit. They whipped him in the name of Jesus. John Lewis and Sarah Chapman, two lovers, were brought to justice for "sitting together on the Lord's day under an apple tree in Goodman Chapman's orchard." And they weren't even doing anything, just sitting there!

Oppressive legalism! And this in a land of freedom?

The Puritans with their Sunday laws missed the meaning of Sabbath rest. When Roger Williams arrived in Massachusetts in 1631, he protested their legislated legalism. Williams claimed civil magistrates had no right to enforce personal religion. The colony condemned him in 1635. He escaped arrest and fled into the snowy forest, finding refuge with the Native Americans. "I would rather live with Christian savages," he wryly commented, "than with savage Christians."

Williams bought land from the Indians and established a new colony dedicated to religious liberty. His settlement, Providence, today is the capital of Rhode Island. Williams welcomed Jews, Catholics, and Quakers as citizens in full and regular standing. Nobody suffered for their faith—or for refusing to believe. But sad to say, later leaders of Rhode Island lapsed into intolerance and legalism and passed a Sunday law in 1679, requiring certain acts and forbidding others.

In that age of coerced obedience, a few had the enlightened courage to stand up for freedom. James Madison, while yet a boy in Virginia, heard a persecuted Baptist minister fearlessly preaching from the window of his prison cell. That day young Madison dedicated his life to fight for freedom of conscience. Tirelessly he toiled with Thomas Jefferson and others to secure the First Amendment in our Bill of Rights. It reads simply and majestically: "Congress shall make no law respecting an establishment of religion, or prohibiting the free exercise thereof." Government must protect religion—but not promote it.

Our founders rejected religion by legislation. So does God. Jesus put it plainly: "Render therefore to Caesar the things that are Caesar's, and to God the things that are God's" (Matthew 22:21). Religious laws and civil laws must be kept separate. What does this mean?

God's Ten Commandments consist of two sections. The first four, including the Sabbath commandment, pertain to our personal relationship with God. Civil government can't enforce matters of personal faith—the first four commandments. But the other six commandments—"Thou shalt not kill," for instance—are civil laws regulating society. These statutes the state must enforce to protect human life and property. But when government intrudes upon one's personal relationship with God, problems abound.

American Sunday Laws

The most blatantly intolerant Colonial American legislation involved Sunday laws. And some of them could really sting the reluctant saint. A Virginia law of 1610 provided that "those who violated the Sabbath or failed to attend church services, morning and afternoon, should on the first offense lose their provisions and allowance of the whole week following; for the second, lose their allowance and be publicly whipped;

and for the third, suffer death" (cited in *American History On-line:* "The Laws of Virginia [1610-1611]").

Death decreed for violating a Sunday law! Right here in America.

Whether or not that draconian law actually was enforced, it no doubt offered powerful motivation to all who might wish to skip church on Sunday, while also warning "heretics" wanting to keep another day holy, such as the Sabbath. Keeping Sunday has always been a trademark of the Christian West. Muslims worship on a different day, Friday. Will Sunday soon become a symbol of Christianity versus Islam? What, then, would happen to those who keep the Sabbath? Just as the Sabbath is located between Sunday and Friday, will those who keep God's seventh day holy find themselves caught in the struggle between a coercive Christianity and a militant Islam?

It happened to the Jews. Keeping a different Sabbath has helped spark anti-Semitism through the centuries. The Middle Ages reveal a long history of opposition to the Sabbath, of which Jesus proclaimed Himself Lord (Matthew 12:8). Will Sabbathkeepers in earth's final crisis likewise be persecuted?

When liberty is lost in this country it won't be because Americans have become bigots and tyrants. Rather, freedoms will be legislated away by well-meaning Christians who know not what they do. They will sacrifice liberties in an attempt to save the Christian West in a time of international crisis. Their goal will be to regain God's favor, but they will discover too late that their efforts were on the wrong side of the Sabbath issue.

Recently Pope John Paul II issued an encyclical urging Sunday laws in the name of social welfare. Requiring one day off seems good for society. Good for the family. Even good for saving energy. But don't believe it! Despite good intentions, Sunday laws always bring intolerance, which in turn brings persecution.

And history will repeat itself. Is the image to the beast forming right now? Zealous Christians already want to enforce the morality of the majority. What will happen next in a time of grave national danger? Let's go back to Revelation 13 and pick up where we left off.

Mark of the Beast

"He causes all, both small and great, rich and poor, free and slave, to receive a mark on their right hand or on their foreheads, and that no one may buy or sell except one who has the mark or the name of the beast, or the number of his name" (Revelation 13:16, 17).

Here we have an international boycott resulting in the mark of the beast, enforced by the image to the beast. How will religious government enforce the mark? Before we explore some clues as to what the mark might be, remember God's seal, His memorial of Creation. Understanding God's seal helps us identify Satan's mark.

In warning us to avoid that mark, the Bible commands us to worship Him who made heaven and earth (Revelation 14:6, 7). So God's creatorship is a key issue in the final conflict. What memorial of Creation has He given us? Could it be that God will use Sabbath rest to measure the loyalty of everyone who chooses to worship Him?

If Sabbath rest in Jesus represents God's seal, can we see what the mark of the beast might be? The Bible says: "They have no rest day or night, who worship the beast and his image" (verse 11). No rest—no Sabbath rest!

DESECRATION, DANGER, DELIVERANCE

At first glance the matter of God's day of rest may seem trivial. But really, the Sabbath controversy isn't between one day or another. Think about it. Are you old enough to remember when Soviet leader Nikita Khrushchev visited America? He took off his shoe and pounded it on the speaker's platform. Amazing! Suppose he had demanded that America abandon its Fourth of July celebrations and memorialize the country on the fifth of July instead? Would Khrushchev have a right to change that day?

Worse yet, suppose America accepted his new day for celebrating American freedom and independence? What would that say about loyalty to our great heritage?

With that in mind, let's go back for a moment to the sixteenth century and the Council of Trent. You may recall that a core issue was the Protestants' insistence on using the Bible and the Bible only. Rome resisted, and they gave this reason: The church had long before shown authority to reinterpret Scripture—because influenced by tradition, it transferred the Sabbath to Sunday.

In his book *Canon and Tradition,* H. J. Holtzmann describes the climactic scene at the Council of Trent. Notice how the decision was reached to give tradition preference in interpreting Scripture. "Finally . . . on the eighteenth of January, 1562, all hesitation was set aside: the archbishop of Reggio made a speech in which he openly declared that tradition stood above Scripture. The authority of the church could therefore not be bound to the authority of the Scriptures, because the church had changed . . . the Sabbath into Sunday, not by the command of Christ, but by its own authority."

So, what carried the day when all hung in the bal-

ance? The fact that the Roman Church had claimed
the authority to change one of God's commandments,
the fourth commandment. The church regarded this
change of worship from Sabbath to Sunday as its mark
of authority.

We see, then, that the Sabbath controversy is not
fundamentally about one day versus another. It's
about leadership. Will we obey God or yield to someone else? Whom will we trust? Where is our loyalty?
The worldwide test may well be coming soon.

From my reading of Scripture, I do not believe that
anyone today has the mark of the beast. God will not
permit anyone to receive that mark until the issues are
out in the open. But when the issues are fully explained
and all have had opportunity to understand and see the
critical and final nature of the matter—then, if we de-
liberately choose to obey a command of men in place
of a command of God and if we yield to coercion and
take the easy way out—we will have marked ourselves,
by our actions, as no longer loyal to God.

The mark will be there—in the forehead if we
believe the propaganda of Satan, or in our hand if we
know it is false but go along with it anyway. Perhaps
we collapse under the pressure and ridicule of the
crowd. Or we succumb to the economic boycott.

The mark may be invisible to other people, but
angels will see it and know where our loyalty lies.
God places His seal only on the forehead, the mind
(Revelation 7:3), never in the hand, for Sabbath rest
isn't forced. It's free and freely chosen. God accepts
only worship that comes from the heart and mind.
Satan doesn't care how he gets his worship. If he can't
win it by choice, he'll grab it by force!

You may find it difficult to conceive of Satan
working through Christian society. It's hard to see how

Bible believers could ever turn to force and coercion. But then we remember the Puritans and their Sunday laws. And before them, the Protestant Reformers during their times of cruel intolerance. Ultimately, the whole earth will join forces against God's faithful remnant. There will even be a death decree.

Faithful Unto Death

Let's recap what we've learned in this chapter. We have reason to expect that America, reacting to some future crisis, will revert to its original roots of colonial intolerance. There will be desperate and determined attempts to force the nation—and, it appears, the entire Christian West—back to God. Persecution will culminate in a death decree for religious dissenters.

Should this surprise us? Jesus warned: "The time is coming that whoever kills you will think that he offers God service" (John 16:2). Evidently persecution typically does not originate among bad people trying to make other people bad but because good people are trying to make other people good. Persecutors can be nice people who take their kids to the park to feed squirrels. They may be filled with zeal for God, thinking it their Christian duty to suppress evil. They fail to recognize that God Himself will not force the conscience.

Racing toward the crisis hour, we cannot ignore or escape the issues at stake. And our decision must be our own. Satan would like to force his way in. Sometimes even loved ones want to enter—loved ones who do not understand. But God Himself won't violate our freedom to choose. He stands at the door of our heart and knocks. He waits for us to accept His love, even though it may cost us jobs, our homes, our dearest earthly relationships—even life itself.

A terrifying prospect, but then we recall the

words of Jesus: "For whoever desires to save his life will lose it, but whoever loses his life for My sake will save it" (Luke 9:24). So "do not fear any of those things which you are about to suffer. Indeed, the devil is about to throw some of you into prison, that you may be tested, and you will have tribulation ten days. Be faithful until death, and I will give you the crown of life" (Revelation 2:10).

Are you willing to be faithful to Christ and His truth, no matter what the cost? God will give you strength if you ask Him.

Chapter 11

ARMAGEDDON'S HOLY WAR

What might it be like to experience Armageddon? Let's imagine a possible scenario.

Suppose it's halftime at the Super Bowl. Millions around the world are watching America's biggest party. Inside the football stadium, 60,000 sports fans whistle and ogle as scantily clad dancers gyrate onstage amid a laser light extravaganza. A fireworks spectacular concludes the show, dazzling the crowd.

Suddenly a huge, blinding explosion, incredible in force, incinerates the stadium. Everyone inside dies instantly. A mushroom cloud forms overhead and hovers above the scene of horror.

As the news sends shock waves through the nation, panic and pandemonium prevail. A nuclear attack within America! Who would do such a thing? Why? What will they do next?

Answers quickly come. A fax arrives at the London *Times* newsroom from somewhere in Lebanon. An obscure Islamic terrorist group is boasting about the bomb, giving all the glory to Allah.

So it is a religious attack. Panic turns to anger. White-hot rage burns against Muslims everywhere—

totally unfair, since the great majority are peaceable, gentle people. Yet innocent Arab taxi drivers waiting for passengers at Washington's Dulles Airport are yanked out of their vehicles and shot.

The terrorists claiming responsibility for the attack declare a jihad, or holy war. It will continue unless America, described as the "Great Satan" and source of the world's worst wickedness, submits to the will of Allah. Meaning what, specifically? All support for Israel must cease and American armed forces stationed in Muslim countries must evacuate.

Naturally, America won't meet those demands, being irrevocably bonded with Israel. Besides, there's no way to abandon its military presence in strategic areas like Kuwait.

"We'll never be held hostage," vows the U.S. president.

So the terror escalates. A bombing here. A poison outbreak there. Some of it high-tech nuclear. Some of it low-tech biotoxins. All of it causes carnage and chaos. The FBI is helpless to stop it. Whenever they seize the members of one jihad cell, other sleeper cells are waiting to spring into action. Death for them holds no fear. And if they can murder some Christian "infidels" as they leave this world, a personal harem of beautiful women awaits them in Paradise.

Holy War

America is engaged in a holy war. Just like the old Crusades, only this time the Christian West is attacked. The president declares a state of national emergency. Preachers flood the airwaves urging—demanding—that America get back to God. There is a general sense that the United States is under divine judgment for pornographic movies, homosexuality, and taking prayer out of public schools.

Politicians join the chorus: "America has sinned! Our only hope is to call upon Heaven, lest we perish. It's a spiritual problem! So we need a spiritual solution."

Miraculous appearances, supposedly of the virgin Mary, deliver further warnings about repentance for Western society. The U.S. president declares a national day of prayer. Congress immediately affirms it. Previously feuding Republicans and Democrats congregate on the steps of the Capitol Building, imploring God to save the nation. Despite fear of public places, a million supplicants crowd the Washington Mall to pray. People prostrate themselves facefirst on the grass and gravel, beseeching God to rescue the nation. Posters rebuke everything from beer to bikinis. Anyone who fails to join the mass prayer crusade is labeled a Muslim sympathizer or atheistic rebel.

The national day of prayer comes and goes, yet the terror continues. Within a week a major Texas oil refinery blows up. Dozens die, and gasoline becomes rationed. A marine helicopter over the American embassy in Saudi Arabia is shot down by a shoulder-fired missile. More dead. Then a smallpox epidemic breaks out in Boston. Since that old killer had been conquered, doctors stopped immunizing against it. But now thousands fall prey to an awful, ancient death.

Meanwhile, the United States becomes a cultural and economic wasteland. Museums and schools are shut. So is the New York Stock Exchange after a bomb threat on Wall Street. Stores are barricaded. Mobs forage for bread and milk. The baseball season is canceled—few would come and risk getting nuked. America is no longer the land of the free and the home of the brave.

Overseas, London is bombed daily, just as in

1940. Brussels, Bonn, Milan, all are under attack. Paris too. And, of course, Jerusalem. Oh, Jerusalem!

The entire Western world is held hostage by shadowy religious fanatics. We're terrified of those wiry young men with fierce dark eyes. Thanks to them, prosperity is past. At stake is the very survival of the Christian West.

Amid this desperation comes another miraculous appearance of "Mary," a huge apparition that fervently appeals: "Let there be peace on earth and goodwill toward humanity. No more terrorism! No more wickedness! Honor God and heed the Holy Father."

Protestant televangelists also promote the pope's plea for Western nations to pass national Lord's Day legislation: "Look how Muslim nations all legislate Friday observance! Until Christian countries return to their heritage and enforce Sunday as fervently, God will not protect us from terrorist attacks."

Popular opinion is overwhelmingly supportive. Anyone who doesn't get on the Sunday bandwagon is labeled either an Islamic sympathizer or an atheist. Jews are made an exception, being considered God's chosen people and immune from His wrath. But everyone else must honor the "Christian Sabbath" or face prison.

From the Oval Office the president appears on TV. On his desk there's a crucifix never seen before as he solemnly announces the invocation of his emergency powers. Instantly democracy becomes a dictatorship. "The purpose is simple survival," he explains. "Radical times require radical measures."

Reflecting historical precedence, few citizens mind their loss of liberty in hopes of restoring national security.

Persecuting Patriots

America, driven to its knees, is praying up a

storm. Panic prevails and rage deepens against anyone refusing to support the national back-to-God movement with its mandate for Sunday sacredness. Preachers condemn Sabbathkeepers as "Achans in the camp," drawing an analogy with the Old Testament Israelite whose lawbreaking caused God's people to die while battling Palestinians. "God's solution was the death penalty for Achan. In our day likewise, God is allowing Palestinian terrorists to murder us and our children until we deal with our own lawbreakers! Every Achan among us also must die, lest the whole nation perish!"

All this fulfills Christ's warning to His disciples: "The time is coming that whoever kills you will think that he offers God service" (John 16:2).

And notice Revelation 12:17: "The dragon [the devil—verse 9] was enraged with the woman [the church, bride of Christ], and he went to make war with the rest of her offspring, who keep the commandments of God and have the testimony of Jesus Christ."

Yes, this is war. Armageddon! It's not primarily a conflict involving professional armies, armored tanks, and fighter jets. Armageddon is a spiritual battle for the heart and soul of the world, the final phase of Satan's plan for this planet—when Christian patriots will persecute.

Let's get some background from the Bible.

A Place Called Armageddon

Just once does Scripture mention the word "Armageddon." It's in the book of Revelation: "For they are the spirits of demons, performing signs, which go out to the kings of the earth and of the whole world, to gather them to the battle of that great day of God Almighty. . . . And they gathered them together to the place called in Hebrew, Armageddon" (Revelation 16:14–16).

This battle is earth's final conflict. Foretold are miracles of deception involving demonic spirits—such as the Marian apparitions already mentioned. (More about this later.) The spiritual armies of God and Satan are at war (Revelation 17:14). Armageddon climaxes the great controversy between good and evil.

Where will this conflict occur? History provides no record of any place called Armageddon, but Scripture offers a hint. The text we read says that the word "Armageddon" comes from Hebrew. In that language, the word combines *har,* meaning "mountain," and *mageddon,* which appears to link with "Megiddo." So the name Armageddon can be understood as "mountain of Megiddo."

The mountain of Megiddo—this gives us something to work with. Thousands of years ago Megiddo was a small but significant fortress city north of Jerusalem near the Plain of Esdraelon. The Bible even calls this plain itself the Plain of Megiddo. This might seem to provide a logical battlefield, but then we recall that Armageddon means not a plain but a mountain.

Confusing! So where is this mountain of Megiddo, a mountain with spiritual significance for the armies of heaven?

Visiting the site of ancient Megiddo could help us analyze Armageddon. Eastward from the Mediterranean port city of Haifa, we follow the Carmel ridge. After passing the northeastern ridge of Carmel, we arrive at the ruins of the ancient city. Towering over the landscape at Megiddo is Mount Carmel.

Perhaps Mount Carmel is our solution. Does it symbolize Mount Megiddo, the scene of Armageddon? What may have happened at Mount

Carmel that would shed light on the New Testament talk about Armageddon?

A Time for Judgment

One unforgettable day almost 3,000 years ago, Mount Carmel hosted a showdown between God and His enemies. Elijah the prophet called the nation to come to the mountain. He challenged the people to decide between true and false worship. Hear his heart-gripping appeal: "How long will you falter between two opinions? If the Lord is God, follow Him; but if Baal, follow him" (1 Kings 18:21).

God won a tremendous victory that day at Mount Carmel. The Israelites repented and reaffirmed their commitment to Him rather than to pagan worship. Unitedly they declared: "The Lord, He is God! The Lord, He is God" (verse 39). After they had taken their stand for God and His government, Elijah executed the leaders who had deceived them.

We see, then, that the summons to Mount Carmel involved judgment—evaluating God and His government. And then a judgment of all who rebelled against Him. Should we expect a similar type of judgment associated with Armageddon? What does Scripture say?

Armageddon will come during the seven plagues at the end of earth's history. Let's learn about these plagues.

The Lord has been patient all these years, sending sunshine and rain even upon His enemies. Suddenly now He sends wrath instead of rain. Why? Has some type of judgment taken place in heaven? Has a verdict been reached? Revelation 11 tells us: "Then the seventh angel sounded: And there were loud voices in heaven, saying, 'The kingdoms of this world have become the kingdoms of our Lord and of His Christ, and He shall reign forever and ever!' And the twenty-four elders who sat before God on their thrones fell on their faces and worshiped God, saying: 'We give You thanks, O Lord God Almighty, the One who is and who was and who is to come, because You have taken Your great power and reigned. The nations were angry, and Your wrath has come, and the time of the dead, that they should be judged, and that You should reward Your servants the prophets and the saints, and those who fear Your name, small and great, and should destroy those who destroy the earth'" (verses 15-18).

An amazing scene! What's happening? A time to be judged, the text tells us—a judgment up in heaven while life continues here on earth. Like at Carmel, God's government must be vindicated before He assumes His authority to punish the wicked.

What's the story behind this judgment?

Way back when Satan was banished from heaven to this earth, he claimed the right to represent our world in the councils of heaven. (The first two chapters of Job, an Old Testament book, tell what happened.) God defended His government in front of the celestial host against the accuser's challenge.

All heaven watched as Satan (at that time this old Hebrew word signified more a position than a proper name) afflicted Job with all sorts of trouble, trying to discourage him from trusting in God. But Job remained faithful—just as God's people will in the last days. Job's trust and loyalty vindicated God against the false charges of the accuser.

What's the purpose of this judgment?

Realizing that loyalty depends upon the ability to trust, God must prove Himself trustworthy. And so

He allows Himself to be audited. This same type of judgment occurs in our business world. A corporation president, charged with dishonesty, may decide to open the books so that every employee can see he or she has been just and fair. The goal is to be trusted. A dishonest leader will do everything possible to prevent such an audit.

God has nothing to hide, so He invites inspection of His government. The apostle Paul understood this aspect of judgment when he wrote: "Let God be found true, though every man be found a liar, as it is written, 'That Thou mightest be justified in Thy words, and mightest prevail when Thou art judged'" (Romans 3:4, NASB).

So God will prevail when He is judged, just as He prevailed in the days of Job. Just as He won His case at Mount Carmel. God convinces the celestial universe that He is worthy of their worship. Satan's challenge is defeated at Armageddon. The kingdoms of the world become God's beyond dispute. Citizens of the universe stand behind Him as He rewards His people and punishes rebellion on earth with the seven last plagues.

Surviving the Plagues

You may know the story of the plagues in Egypt just before the Exodus of God's people from their land of bondage. What saved them from the death angel? Blood on their doorposts. God promised, "When I see the blood, I will pass over you; and the plague shall not be on you to destroy you when I strike the land of Egypt" (Exodus 12:13).

The blood—that's what counts! The blood of Jesus. Protected by our Savior's sacrifice, we are safe from the punishing plagues.

ARMAGEDDON'S HOLY WAR

Once every person decides for life or death, earth's harvest will be ripe for judgment. All who trust in Jesus and keep His commandments are sealed for eternal life. And those who refuse God's salvation will receive the mark of the beast, as we studied.

In the book of Revelation, just before the final plagues, God sends three angels with special worldwide warnings. Each angel proclaims one part of God's final admonition to the human race. These angels, of course, are symbolic of their messages. They don't literally fly overhead with loudspeakers.

Here is the first warning: "Then I saw another angel flying in the midst of heaven, having the everlasting gospel to preach to those who dwell on the earth—to every nation, tribe, tongue, and people—saying with a loud voice, 'Fear God and give glory to Him, for the hour of His judgment has come; and worship Him who made heaven and earth, the sea and springs of water'" (Revelation 14:6, 7).

Here's the everlasting gospel, the same message of salvation dear to the apostle Paul and to Martin Luther. Now, however, there's a new urgency, because "the hour of His judgment has come"—a judgment like that at Mount Carmel long ago. And did you notice the very language of the Sabbath commandment here, calling the world to worship its Creator?

Next comes the second angel, warning about Babylon—organized religious abomination and oppression. Finally, the third angel sounds the alarm about the mark of the beast with its false worship, symbolized by observance of the ancient day of the sun.

So it is that every soul decides for life or death. The disobedient receive wrath. After the seventh and last plague, Christ returns to airlift His people from Armageddon.

As the New International Commentary on the New Testament confirms: "Har-Mageddon is symbolic of the final overthrow of all the forces of evil by the might and power of God. . . . God will emerge victorious and take with him all who have placed their faith in him" (*The Book of Revelation,* New International Commentary on the New Testament [Grand Rapids: Eerdmans Publishing Co., 1977], p. 302).

So we see again that Armageddon is a showdown between truth and error, loyalty to either God or the powers of evil. While the armies of the earth may be fighting, the dominant activity of Armageddon is a spiritual conflict with fierce deceptions involving the antichrist.

Let's dig a bit deeper.

Deceiving Spirits

Revelation 16 speaks of the "spirits of demons, performing signs, which go out to the kings of the earth and of the *whole world, to gather them* to the battle of that great day of God Almighty. . . . And they gathered them together to the place called . . . Armageddon" (Revelation 16:14-16).

Mark those words—the whole world will be unified through satanic miracles involving personifying spirits. How might this come about?

Consider what happened in the village of Fatima, Portugal, one spring day in 1917. Three shepherd children were tending their flock midday when sudden lightning burst through the cloudless sky. The children fled in fear. A glorious woman materialized in the sky and stopped them. She identified herself as Mary, mother of Christ, commissioned by God to warn the church and the world.

One prediction was that Russia would spread its

errors throughout the world but then become converted. Many Catholics believe that the fall of Euro-Communism has provided Russia with religious opportunities that will result in its eventual Christianization. Other Fatima predictions have also apparently been fulfilled. But does this prove that God inspired the messages and then orchestrated them?

Soon after the Fatima appearances, a local Catholic priest initially suggested that the three shepherd children, though undeniably sincere, might have been deceived by a satanic visitation. In other words, Satan was using them as bait to deceive the world. Could such a thing happen? Was this priest correct in raising such doubts? Should we scrutinize the source of miraculous occurrences before accepting them as coming from God?

Suppose those Fatima children really saw a supernatural being. Would this prove that Mary herself had appeared miraculously? Remember, Jesus warned earth's final generation that "false prophets will rise and show great signs and wonders to deceive, if possible, even the elect" (Matthew 24:24).

So we must test miraculous spirits by the Bible. To qualify as being from Christ, the messages from Fatima and everything else must synchronize with Scripture.

Throughout the years, especially recently, Catholics of all ages and backgrounds have reported sightings of Mary. Hundreds of them, all over the world. The messages share a common thread. All are urgent calls for repentance and prayer to avoid divine chastisement.

Well, who could argue with a call to repentance? Unfortunately, other elements of these messages raise serious questions. Again and again we hear references to the "immaculate heart" of Mary. Scripture affirms her as a woman of humility and integrity, but was

Christ's mother "immaculate" in terms of divine righteousness? No. Mary herself acknowledged her need for a personal Savior when she proclaimed: "My soul magnifies the Lord, and my spirit has rejoiced in God my Savior. . . . Holy is His name" (Luke 1:46-49).

"God is my Savior," Mary testified. "His name is holy." Nevertheless, many are looking to Mary as a sinless mediator to approach God. But the Bible teaches that "there is one God and one Mediator between God and men, the Man Christ Jesus" (1 Timothy 2:5). The exaltation of Mary seems almost unbounded. Historically, her images have been objects of disobedience to the second commandment. (The second commandment is deleted in all Catholic catechisms. By splitting the tenth commandment into two commandments, they manage to retain the number 10. [See Exodus 20:4-6, 17.] We have already seen how the fourth commandment regarding the Sabbath was corrupted.)

And now there is a worldwide campaign to exalt her to the status of co-redeemer with Jesus. This is well-intentioned, no doubt, but blasphemous, since Christ alone is our salvation, our sole Savior.

Unifying the World

Marian apparitions are becoming more and more frequent around the globe, with increasing publicity and influence. Could these appearances be instrumental in unifying the whole world in counterfeit Christian worship, as predicted in the Armageddon passage of Revelation 16?

What about Muslims? One intriguing detail about Fatima is that the founder of Islam, Muhammad, had a beloved daughter by that name. Muslims might see this as an indication from Allah that these apparitions are for them, too. The Koran even acknowledges that Mary is the highest woman in heaven. (Actually, the real Mary is not in heaven but is sleeping in the grave with all the rest of God's saints, awaiting the coming of Jesus to awaken them from death. See 1 Thessalonians 4:16-18 and 1 Corinthians 15:22, 23, 51-55.)

As for Jews, what effect will these apparitions have upon them? The ABC network telecast *Good Morning America Sunday* recently aired a fascinating segment called "The Cult of Mary." Here are excerpts from a Jewish author, Naomi Wolf: "All over the world, Mary and apparitions are appearing in Rwanda and Sarajevo, to people who are Catholic and not Catholic, like an apparition in North Africa to a bunch of Muslims. . . . I'm an observant Jew. And what strikes me as a non-Catholic is that when these apparitions appear to people, . . . her message is a political message of peacemaking, of reconciliation. And what is amazing to me as a non-Catholic is that she's actually starting to say all religions are equally valid, all religions are a path to God. That's quite moving to me. . . . And that means extending a hand across the divisions of race and across divisions of religion. . . . And it means being open to each other's spiritual traditions" (Naomi Wolf, interview, "The Cult of Mary," *Good Morning America Sunday* [February 7, 1999], electronic transcript, www.abcnews.com).

An amazing testimony! Marian apparitions are appearing to Muslims and influencing even an observant Jew to seek unity and reconciliation through a shared experience in the miraculous.

How would India and the other homelands of Eastern religions react? They acknowledge many divine expressions of the "universal god force" and have no reason to reject these new apparitions. The same is true for tribal Africa, indigenous South Americans, and people of Oceania. In America, Western Europe, Australia, and New Zealand, New Age adherents already believe in the miraculous. As for Christians themselves all around the world, remember that Jesus said the deceptions before His coming would be so fierce that even true believers would be tested. Superficial saints surely will be swept away with the satanic delusions.

The Supreme Deception

We can probably expect further miraculous masquerades of Mary, but the supreme deception will be a counterfeit appearance of Christ Himself, personified by Satan. As we saw in chapter 3 of this book, this will be the ultimate deception of the antichrist in his various expressions throughout Christian history.

Ponder the following description of prophetic insight from Ellen G. White, written a century ago, about how a counterfeit christ might appear at the climax of Armageddon. "Fearful sights of a supernatural character will soon be revealed in the heavens, in token of the power of miracle-working demons. . . . As the crowning act in the great drama of deception, Satan himself will personate Christ. . . . In different parts of the earth, Satan will manifest himself among men as a majestic being of dazzling brightness. . . . The shout of triumph rings out upon the air: 'Christ has come! Christ has come!' The people prostrate themselves in adoration before him, while he lifts up his hands and pronounces a blessing upon them, as Christ blessed His disciples when He was upon the earth" (*The Great Controversy*, p. 624).

Imagine the devil, impersonating Jesus Christ, appearing in Jerusalem, perhaps appearing with an apparition of Mary. The impostor of our Savior would probably bless children, heal the multitudes, and promote world peace through the total cessation of terrorism and renunciation of nuclear weapons. The message of unity and love would be accompanied by a firm warning to enforce the day of worship honoring the Resurrection. Such a deception would be almost irresistible.

Even for Muslims? Although many sincere adherents to Islam may hate Christianity, many Muslims actually expect Jesus to return as a prophet to Jerusalem. So they are vulnerable to the appearance of a miraculous antichrist. Some atheists may see in such an event undeniable and irresistible evidence of the supernatural and join the ranks of the deceived.

So Satan, appearing personally and personating Christ as the final deception of the antichrist, could thus deceive the planet. Convinced by demonic miracles, the whole world could ultimately convert to counterfeit worship and declare the death penalty for those who stubbornly refuse to honor the "Lord's Day"—Babylon's heritage from pagan sun worship. The nations unite to do battle, not against each other but against God's faithful, commandment-keeping remnant.

The Great Tribulation

"And there shall be a time of trouble, such as never was since there was a nation, even to that time. And at that time Your people shall be delivered, every one who is found written in the book" (Daniel 12:1).

Yes, there will be a great tribulation just before Christ's coming. That's the bad news. The good news is that God's loyal people—the genuine Trib Force—will be delivered, every one of them written in the Lamb's book of life.

Are you willing to stand up and be counted among God's faithful followers?

Chapter 12

RAYFORD'S LAST CHANCE

Rayford missed the rapture and was left behind. So were Chloe, Buck, Bruce, Tsion, David, and the other familiar and endearing *Left Behind* personalities. They all enjoyed a second chance and took full advantage of it, as we read in the best-selling fictional series.

Unfortunately, the notion of a second chance is itself fictional, as we have seen from the Bible. When Jesus returns for His saints, anyone left behind is left dead. As it was in the days of Noah. As it was when fire rained down upon Sodom.

"Behold, now is the accepted time; behold, now is the day of salvation" (2 Corinthians 6:2). So if you want to join the Trib Force, you had better do it now.

God is building His team. Would you like to join? How?

Jesus said: "My sheep hear My voice, and I know them, and they follow Me" (John 10:27). The Good Shepherd speaks to us through the Bible. We hear His voice calling when He reveals new truth, stretching us out of our comfort zone and into His courageous zone.

Will you pass the test of truth? The choice is

yours. And it is a choice being made today, either for life or for death.

A word of encouragement: When your faith is tested in obeying Bible truth, you can thank God for an opportunity to prepare for earth's final crisis. During that time of tribulation soon to come, each soul will be tested to the limit. By taking your stand for truth now, you can settle it with God that, come what may, you will be faithful—even unto death, if necessary.

Taking a Stand

Meet Humberto Noble Alexander, a Seventh-day Adventist pastor in the New York area. With his sparkling eyes and exuberant laughter, nobody would guess he spent 22 years in a loathsome Communist dungeon, all for the sake of his faith in Christ. Tested to the limit, his faith not only survived but thrived. Noble became the unofficial pastor of an interdenominational group of worshipers.

"One evening as the little band gathers for worship, Noble notices a guard quietly counting the attendees. Just as they complete singing a hymn, a soldier explodes inside and orders all worshipers outside. 'Line up!' he barks.

"Everyone knows their punishment—the dreaded isolation chamber. The guard stalks up and down the line and shouts: 'I see only 20 of you here. There were 30 inside. You're 10 short!'

"Noble prays hard for strength. As leader, his punishment will be the worst.

"The guard keeps yelling for the missing men. Meanwhile, other prisoners are watching from the back of the courtyard. They hear the desperate guard threaten: 'If those 10 inmates don't appear immediately, I'm going to punish the entire cell block.'

THE GREAT TRIBULATION —IT'S HERE!

Antichrist Nicolae Carpathia, who died and rose again, now rules the world. He desecrates Jerusalem's new temple by shedding the blood of a pig on its altar. Blood flows freely in New York, London, Rome, as the world marches toward Armageddon.

But is this popular scenario reality, or red herring? Will the antichrist be a blatant blasphemer, like Nicolae Carpathia? Or will he be a trusted Christian leader, a wolf in sheep's clothing, operating within the "temple" of God—His church?

False teaching about the end can be dangerous. According to the *Left Behind* scenario, for example, you can party now and pray later. Wait till those boring believers disappear, then repent. But will those who miss the first rapture have a second chance, or only a second death? What about the rebuilding of the temple? Will America become a persecuting power? What is the mark of God and the mark of the beast? And how can we be protected in the last days?

In this hard-hitting exposé of the *Left Behind* fantasy, Martin Weber exposes the myth of the rapture and shows what the Bible actually teaches about Armageddon, the tribulation, the antichrist, and the Second Coming. You will relive critical moments in history and dig deep into Scripture to discover the startling truth about your future.

That truth is your safeguard. Just keep your mind open—and your Bible close by.

As pastor, associate editor of *Ministry*, and scriptwriter for *It Is Written*, Martin Weber has conducted Bible seminars on five continents. Currently he is pursuing a doctorate in British Columbia. Previous books include *Hurt, Healing, and Happy Again;* and *My Tortured Conscience*.

ISBN 0-8280-1706-9

9 780828 017060

REVIEW AND HERALD®
PUBLISHING ASSOCIATION